Mission
on the
Margins

Mission
on the
Margins

Mary Beasley

The Lutterworth Press
Cambridge

The Lutterworth Press
P.O. Box 60
Cambridge
CB1 2NT

British Library Cataloguing in Publication Data:
A catalogue record is available from the British Library.

ISBN 0 7188 2966 2

Printed in Great Britain by
The Guernsey Press Co. Ltd., Guernsey, Channel Islands

Contents

Foreword by Kenneth Leech

Christian Churches have a long record of concern for 'the poor'. They have done good to 'the poor', fed and clothed 'the poor', campaigned on behalf of 'the poor', been advocates of 'the poor'. But often 'the poor have remained 'out there', the recipients, even the victims, of 'our' pastoral care. In recent years this kind of division between the 'doers' and the 'done to' has got much worse, as our political regime has led to increased exclusion, and, I fear, as many Churches have become more remote and managerial, more cut off from those who are most in need.

I believe that we are increasingly labelling whole sections of society by use of terms such as 'the poor', 'the underclass', and so on. It is a dehumanising mechanism, filled with condescension and at times contempt. It destroys human relationships and encourages the worst kind of paternalism. The fact that pastoral ministry can, and often does, dehumanise was recognised a hundred years ago by William Booth, founder of the Salvation Army, and it remains a serious danger for us today.

In the last few years it has been an enormous privilege for me to have been involved in helping to create a national network in Britain called 'Mission on the Margins'. This network grew from the work of my remarkable friend, Mary Beasley, the author of this book. Mary, a disabled woman and former social worker, had been working with homeless and alcoholic people, as well as with other marginal groups, in Birmingham for some years. Through writing a university thesis on her work, she came into contact with a wide range of people doing similar work in other towns and cities – including myself – and so the network was born. It has brought together a diverse group of people from all the Churches, including many who themselves are marginal to the institution, who share a common commitment to service and to advocacy on behalf of those who have been cast off or rejected by the system.

The work of Mission on the Margins brings to the surface some important warnings for the Church in the twenty-first century. One is the inextricable link between the response to poor people and the humanity of the whole community. Liberation theologians such as Jon Sobrino have stressed that to stand before poor people with honesty is a first step towards humanisation of all human beings. Yet so much ministry, like so much politics, is directed towards the respectable, secure and well-behaved, where success and financial stability are more likely.

I commend Mary's book with a sense of urgency. It is not comfortable reading. Indeed I hope it will disturb its readers and cause them to examine their own commitment. More than this, I hope that it will lead to a realignment of those Christians who put the demands of justice and mercy before their own promotion, success or status. At a time when security, comfort and contentment preoccupy many, it is important that we take Mary's story seriously, and that we act upon it.

KENNETH LEECH
St Botolph's Church, Aldgate
February 1997

Preface

This book began life as an MPhil thesis 'A theological reflection on an apostolate among street people', but has been extensively revised to make it relevant to the thinking Christian. I would like to make two points, firstly concerning the terms I have used, and secondly an acknowledgement of those who have contributed to the work described.

1. An explanation of the term 'apostolate' is given in the Introduction but, although I make a passing reference to the reason for the term 'street people' this requires further explanation. Since I finished the thesis I have heard that in some quarters that the term has become a pejorative one.

My original reason for using it was because the people themselves were using it and their interpretation accurately described those with whom I was concerned. It includes people who have 'dropped out' of the mainstream of society, have broken any ties they may have had with family and established community, either because they are the product of broken homes, often having been in care, or because of a subsequent breakdown in relationships. Thus the term 'street people' is more concerned with the overall social situation than with details of material circumstances.

The term 'single homeless and rootless' is used by some welfare agencies. By definition this implies that their situation is one of not having a stable relationship with a partner, not having a permanent home, and lacking a network of links with family and community. It can therefore be taken as being almost synonymous with the more popular term 'street people', apart from the fact that the latter may not be technically homeless.

The term 'Fourth World' is also used to include street people. This term is used to include all who are alienated from the mainstream of society: single-parent families;

travellers; and people who are disadvantaged in various ways. While it is used on occasion, particularly in later quotations from others, it describes much wider situations than those included in the term 'street people'.

Another term, which is used by Kenneth Leech and others, is 'marginal'. In *Care and Conflict* he states that

The term 'marginal' had originally been used by the Chicago sociologist Robert Park in 1928 about the position of ghetto Jews in the USA. Glass used it in 1960 about communities which were cut off from resources and from power, locked into conditions of social inferiority and insecurity.

The term 'underclass' is used where the sources under discussion have used it.

I use the term 'marginal' where I am discussing the more general position of those who fall outside the social structures; I use the term 'street people' where there is a need to be more specific as to the particular people to whom I am referring.

2. The MPhil thesis described a journey; part of it had taken place before I began the research, but part was the result of the earlier stages of the research. I therefore travelled some distance on my own journey during the course of the research, and I would like to thank fellow travellers and those from whom I learnt so much.

First and foremost, this book could not have been rooted in real life without the first-hand experience of those whom I met in the 'urban jungle'. Also people in pastoral and apostolic work there, with an ability to reflect theologically on it, have been among the most helpful of fellow travellers; I am particularly grateful to staff and postgraduate students in the Theology Department at Birmingham University. This book has been a joint effort which could not have happened without the encouragement of others.

Introduction

Telephone calls requiring immediate action in the middle of the night are not part of most people's working life, unless they work in the emergency services. That this was not an uncommon occurrence for me was symptomatic of the disrupted lives of those among whom I moved.

One such incident involved a girl who had previously been in the drug and prostitution scene. She had tried to break with it, but had subsequently moved from one unstable partnership to another. When such relationships went through a stormy patch, having no other home, she would drift around her old haunts. On this occasion she had been found by her former pimp, who had made threats as to what would happen if she did not go back to 'work' for him. Had she not had somewhere where she could stay till she either returned to her partner or found somewhere else to live, she would have had difficulty avoiding the pimp, and his threats.

I had previously been in local authority social work. There we were addressing the needs of children committed to the care of the local authority by the juvenile court, or otherwise 'at risk', the mentally ill and those with 'learning difficulties', the elderly and those with physical disabilities.

But this left big gaps, particularly where young people who had been in care were concerned. A question that concerned me was what happens to a vulnerable young person when they reach the age of eighteen if their parents are not on the scene? In the seventies, when I was first in social work, no statutory service was responsible for these young people once they were eighteen. If there was a mental breakdown, or the young person had a child considered to be 'at risk', Social Services might have taken action; if an offence was committed, the Probation Service might have been involved. But, short of such a crisis, the young person had no adult to whom they could turn.[1]

Most young people, when they leave home, can expect

ongoing support from their families, yet in those days there were young people, in need of more support than most, going out into the big wide world with no-one to provide that.

Young people who had been in care kept in contact after I left Social Services, particularly when difficulties arose. People from unstable backgrounds are more likely to form partnerships with those in a similar situation, and these are likely to break down, with the result that at least one would have been on the streets had there been nowhere where they could stay and pick up the pieces. At one time I was in contact with several young couples where one or both of the partners had been in care; the difficulties they experienced were such that as often as not I had one of them in the house while they sorted out the latest problem in the relationship with the other.

The alcohol and drug abusers whom I got to know were another side of the question. Most had been in care, or otherwise came from broken homes; they had found that alcohol or drugs could deaden the emotional pain of rejection. They might go through residential alcohol or drug rehabilitation programmes; while there, they did well, but once they were back in their old surroundings their low self-esteem would lead to loneliness, depression – and a return to substance abuse or other symptoms of the underlying need.

The symptoms were being treated but not the underlying causes. This was satisfactory for those who had supportive families to return to, such as the businessman who had taken to excessive drinking under pressure, or the teenager from a stable family who had been tempted to experiment with drugs and then become hooked. I also found that some facilities expressed a preference for those who had a good prognosis, on the grounds that work with them was more cost effective. But for the person for whom *the* problem was the lack of such family support, it was not enough.

The girl involved in prostitution was an example of this. When I first knew her, she was abusing drugs. Her mother was an alcoholic; her father had committed suicide when she was eleven, and she was the one who found him. She began to use drugs and play truant from school in her early teens, and was sent to what was then known as an 'approved school' – a facility to which young people might be sent in those days if they needed closer supervision than was provided in ordinary children's homes.

The person who had been supplying her with drugs was awaiting her on her discharge – only then she had to earn her drugs through prostitution. She gave up drugs – for a while – but soon these were replaced by alcohol. After a brief spell of relative stability she became anorexic, and was also being treated for depression.

This demonstrated the need to look at the underlying cause, not only the visible symptom.

An overall picture was emerging. The 'caring' services as a whole were focused more on specific problems than on the whole person. What is more, with this emphasis on problem solving there was a reluctance to take on situations which did not have an apparent solution, as the following episode illustrates.

'If this girl runs away from home, I suggest you forget about her. There is nothing more that can be done for her', was the advice given me when I went to meet a new teenage 'client' whose social worker I was to be.

At fourteen the girl had run through all the options then open to the social services department in whose care she had been placed by the juvenile court. Her final port of call had also been an approved school. The officer in charge had decided that the school could no longer cope after she had set fire to the secure unit to which she had been confined for disturbed behaviour. A child psychiatrist had suggested that she should be sent to the adolescent unit at Rampton, one of the secure psychiatric hospitals.

My team leader wisely felt that that was too extreme a measure and that we would have to take the only other course of action open to us. That was to send the girl 'home on trial', which meant that while the care order remained in effect, the girl would live with one of her divorced parents under my supervision.

The attitude of the officer in charge set me thinking. He had no hope for the girl's future; that pessimism may well have been communicated, albeit unwittingly, to her. How is anyone, who has started as emotionally disturbed, likely to respond to the message that there is no hope? The lack of self-worth that comes from the absence of caring, affirming relationships in childhood is likely to be compounded by such attitudes.

There were indeed a few problems after she was removed from the approved school – and she did run away from home. But, significantly, she blossomed out when placed in a small unit for adolescent girls run by nuns. Initially I had dismissed this suggestion, on the grounds that the nuns might not have the expertise to cope with her; after all the rejections in her life I did not want her to experience another. But the quality of relationships in the unit appeared to provide her with the stability she had previously lacked.

Agencies such as Social Services were looking at the tip of the iceberg, but not at the submerged mass – of people who were hurting because they were isolated from normal social links with family and community which provide the affirmation that is essential to emotional health. In referring to them I use the term 'street people', in the sense that they use it themselves, to describe people who, if not literally homeless, lack links with family and community.

Christianity emphasises the unique worth of each individual; within this people adrift in the world such as orphans, strangers and the poor, have a special place. Yet, as will be apparent particularly in Chapter II, many people who initiated an outreach from a Church base experienced difficulties with the Church concerned. Those within it felt uncomfortable when they found people from a different background in their midst, and the latter felt equally ill at ease.

The Salvation Army's founder, William Booth, never intended to break away from existing Churches. Yet, when he began his outreach to destitute people he found that they were not welcome in the Churches, and they themselves felt ill at ease there. I found this pattern to be repeated in a number of agencies. In particular, I had spent time with an agency in New York which had an outreach to street people from which had arisen a rehabilitation program for drug, mainly heroin, addicts. Being aware of the gap between people on the streets and those in the Churches, they wished to look at some of the issues involved. They concluded that street people should be recognised as a distinct social group, in the same way as are Third World communities, in that neither relates to the mainly middle-class European culture of the existing Churches.

There was a parallel here with the three-stage expansion of the early Church: the Jewish tradition of the Jerusalem Church; Paul's travels in the Gentile world; and what Vincent Donovan calls the 'global stage', covering the third world and also those in the first world outside the predominantly middle-class culture of its Churches.[2] Of particular interest was the experience of the apostle Paul. As he moved out among the Gentiles he came into conflict with the Jerusalem Church which expected the new converts to conform to Jewish law and culture. His pattern was to found Churches which related to the local culture in which they took root; for example, the Corinthian Church was established in a cosmopolitan community where many came from a disrupted lifestyle – the 'sin of Corinth' being synonymous with prosti-tution – yet he met them where they were, rather than insisting on an adoption of Jewish law and customs.

Contemporary Churches seemed to anticipate that converts from a different social and cultural milieu would conform to that of those who constituted the membership of such Churches. As with Paul's ministry there was a need to distinguish between what was essential to the gospel, and the cultural 'baggage' that had become part and parcel of the existing Churches.

Projects were needed which were free to meet people on their own social and cultural ground. Expectation that they might be integrated into existing Church institutions was not in line with the Church's expansion

I therefore set up the 'Birmingham project' with a Church-based social-work agency, to provide a people-centred

Christian presence recognising the social and cultural gap.

A former brothel might not be regarded as a 'desirable residence'. Yet, when offered this by the housing association I had approached for an inner-city property, I decided that if one was to take the 'incarnational' approach seriously, then this was the place. This was not only physically accessible to the city centre and places where people who were adrift tended to gather, but the unpretentious setting, combined with working on an expenses plus pocket money basis, as opposed to a normal salary meant that my lifestyle would not be as removed from inner-city dwellers as would normally be the case with people working on a more conventional, professional basis.

I describe the project as an 'apostolate' to distinguish it from social work. This is a term particularly used in Roman Catholic circles to describe work which establishes a Christian presence in a new area for the Church's activity, derived from the role of the apostles.[3] J. Hoekendijk says in *The Church Inside Out* that

Apostolate in our situation presupposes that ecclesiastically one is willing to enter no-man's land. This means that a great freedom is offered to really identify oneself with others, even when their ideology is rejected.[4]

The object of this project was to find ways to enter the 'no man's land' of people on the streets in order to be present to them, and to involve people from the Churches in this.

Once the project was established, I felt the need to look further into the theological questions raised by it. I had spent years at the 'coalface' and wanted the opportunity to stand back and look at what was going on. I wanted to look at the experience of others in similar work and see what else could be learned from the parallels between this and Third World 'mission' situations.

A difference in emphasis became apparent. Some agencies were primarily concerned with conveying a message, or performing 'works of mercy'; although there was some acknowledgement of a different social group, this was in order that the latter could receive what was being communicated. On the other hand, there were those who recognised a need for two-way communication; they found that they were receiving as much as they were giving, and hence were entering into dialogue with those among whom they were working. This is comparable to the distinction which Hoekendijk makes between 'proclamation', likened to the sermon, and 'communication', which involves entering into the situation of another.

But few were prepared to build relationships where such communication was possible. At first sight it might have been explained by stereotyped views of 'street people'. But I found there was a parallel in the way in which other marginal people were regarded; those in the Churches were prepared to provide material help, but did not wish to have them in their communities. There was a block to communication to be investigated.

We use the term 'urban jungle' to describe the more disrupted areas of cities. I therefore looked at the significance of the 'forest' and the 'stranger' in symbolism and mythology. The term forest is, in some ancient usage, interchangeable with the wilderness, which in turn is similar to the desert. This demonstrated an area of the unknown, of which the 'stranger' is the personification, contrasting with the normal social structures. While this may be a source of threat, it may also be a place of power and encounter with God.

The desert, with its hermits, played a key role in Western Christianity, both as a place of renewal and providing a critique of the wider social structures. Having recognised a symbolic link between the desert and the 'urban jungle' there was the question as to a possible relationship between the voluntarily marginalised inhabitants of the former, and the involuntarily marginalised inhabitants of the latter.

'In what way are you being evangelised by the poor?' I was asked when I first approached Birmingham University with a view to doing a research degree based on my work. The extent to which I, and others, might be so evangelised by people on the margins of society was something I had not anticipated at the outset.

I. From Bridle Path to City Street

A childhood spent among the 'unspeakable in pursuit of the uneatable', as Oscar Wilde called the fox hunting fraternity, might seem an unlikely background for life and work in the inner city. Yet, it is not as far-fetched as it appears; in many remoter rural areas there used to be a community spirit in which helping neighbours was taken for granted.

I can recall my parents asking me to take Christmas presents to some children of my age, eight or nine, whose mother had recently died. They lived a couple of miles away and the snow was too thick for either a bicycle or a pony; my complaints were met with a lecture about the virtues of Good King Wenceslaus, so off I set – on shanks's pony.

Relationships in country communities were indeed very paternalistic, but there was a recognition that the 'haves' had a responsibility towards the 'have-nots'. Most people now would question the assumption made in a hymn which portrayed 'the rich man in his castle and the poor man at his gate' as part of God's plan. But it illustrates a difference which I found between urban and rural society. The 'haves' were not such by their own effort, but by inherited privilege; the 'have-nots' were not such as a result of lack of ability.

There is a marked contrast here with the greater social mobility of urban society. Those who have 'made it' have done so either through their own or their parents' hard work; there is a tendency to think that anyone else could do the same, and conversely that those who are on the streets have chosen that lifestyle, or have been too idle to support themselves – an attitude which reflects the distinction made by some between the 'deserving' and the 'undeserving' poor.

My own initiation into inner-city work was preceded by a series of challenges. As a 'country girl' I had grown up among people who thought that the British ruling classes knew what was best for the rest of the world.

A lady's maid in a country house was an unlikely catalyst. On a weekend visit to friends in my late teens, I found myself being looked after by a girl of my own age. That I should be lying in bed while she prepared my clothes for the day, and washed my dirty underwear from the previous day, made me feel uncomfortable. I don't say that I immediately went off and joined the most politically radical organisation I could find, but it started the process of questioning.

Life in a newly independent East African country was another challenge to belief in the supremacy of the British way of life. It necessitated meeting people where they were, not where one was oneself, and listening to what made them tick. This was illustrated by the question as to what language one spoke. The majority of expatriates assumed that, because English was widely spoken, there was no need to learn Swahili. Yet this reflected a reluctance to identify with the local culture and way of life; even a token gesture of learning a little of the local language was appreciated for the statement it made.

This might at first seem a far cry from being among people who had dropped out of society, but it was valuable in terms of not taking one's own way of life as being the standard for others, and paved the way for looking at mission to 'Fourth World' people in a similar light as that to Third World people.

None of this was *by itself* a training for what was to come, but it did challenge preconceived ideas, and paved the way for an openness which might not otherwise have been there. The main training came from the people among whom I worked themselves.

'Street people' and their stories

Two things struck me. Firstly, the street people were looking for something over and above skilled professional help; they wanted someone who accepted them as they were and helped them to believe in their own potential. The girls who came to stay in my home were every bit as intelligent and competent as I was. Yet they had no idea that they had the ability to continue their education, get qualifications, and so have better prospects in what was already a rapidly contracting employment market. They had such a low view of their own worth as human beings and their gifts that such a thought had not entered their heads.

This devaluing of themselves was the result of early childhood rejection. As an inexperienced social worker I did not think I had much to offer, but was amazed to find how much difference simple friendship and acceptance made; it provided something of what they had missed in normal family life.

Secondly, this pattern, of emotional deprivation and low self-esteem, could lead to various 'symptoms'. In the Introduction I described a girl who at different stages had problems with drug and alcohol abuse, anorexia, and depression. As I worked with drug abusers, alcoholics, the mentally ill and offenders, the pattern was similar; what was significant was not what symptom they presented, but the factors that underlay the symptoms. 'B's' story illustrates this.

His mother was a single parent in Ireland at a time when there was a greater stigma attached to unmarried mothers. She put him in an orphanage when he was very young and visited him once a month, but this did not appear to mean much to him; he says she was like a stranger. He only saw his father four times, and then not till he was in his teens. When he was about ten he was transferred to a 'community home with education' which he described as a repressive, regimented regime. He said that he was often beaten for wetting the bed and commented that the brothers in the religious order which ran the home constantly watched the boys; this may have contributed towards him being very withdrawn and suspicious.

There does not seem to have been any significant adult in his life. Even when he heard his mother had died of cancer soon after he left school, the only feeling he seems to have had about it was emptiness. He did, however, think of what might have been if he had tried to find his mother and father when he left school. He was later sent to work in a variety of places, doing kitchen work and odd-jobbing, but never stayed anywhere very long. He became depressed and a loner at a very early age.

He came to England in his early twenties. At first he tried living in hostels, but was always asked to leave because of his bed-wetting so took to sleeping rough. He began drinking heavily as this helped him overcome his shyness with people. At some stage he had what resembled an epileptic fit – it is common for people who have been drinking heavily for a sustained period to develop epilepsy – for which he was prescribed phenobarbitone and other epilepsy drugs.

He took to mixing these with alcohol; eventually he was drinking cider mixed with wine, and surgical spirits. What work he did in the early days was mostly casual; his drinking meant that he could not hold down a regular job. He was frequently charged with being drunk and disorderly, and was often in prison for this. On one occasion, he also did eighteen months for robbery.

The only meaningful relationship he had was when he was about thirty-five with a girlfriend whom he describes as the only bright light in his life. They lived together for a while but she missed her home town and disappeared, leaving him in a deep depression when he could not find her.

He made more than one serious suicide attempt following this. On the last occasion he was found in a park by police who charged him with being drunk and incapable. The court made a hospital order and he spent a year in a local psychiatric hospital, after which he was sent to a council flat. His self-neglect continued; he was no longer capable of work of any description, was living entirely on 'dole' money, most of which was spent on cheap drink, such as surgical spirits.

Self-hatred may still be an overriding factor even for those with some qualifications and work experience. 'R' was a gifted person; he had obtained four 'A' levels, which would be no mean achievement now, but one which would have marked him as a potential university candidate when he took them in the 1960s. He had played in an orchestra and worked on a newspaper, but his low self-image led to a destructive lifestyle – and ultimately death.

There was an early breakdown in family relationships. R spent much of his time away from home and considerable pain could be heard in his voice when he mentioned his family; when he died they could not be traced.

He gave up heroin without treatment or rehabilitation but this was replaced by alcohol abuse. Being a musician, he could go into pubs and play the piano in return for drinks. He, too, developed epilepsy, and combined alcohol with his epilepsy medication. Physical complications arose from his substance abuse and he was often in hospital after drinking bouts. When I first met him, he had had neither a job nor his own home for some time. He was a loner, and could not cope with even the relatively low-key group activities in a rehabilitation hostel for alcoholics where he stayed for a while.

He was, when sober, very concerned about his drinking, partly because of the physical risks, but seemed unable to identify or deal with the situations that sparked it off. He said that he would go out, with no intention of getting drunk, but then on impulse would go into a pub or off-licence, and this would be the beginning of a long spell of drinking. He went into deep depressions, during which he was unable to communicate with others; it was these bouts which sparked off his drinking 'binges'.

Christmas is a time when many on Skid Row reach a low point, probably because of the emphasis on families at such a time. This happened to R and on an exceptionally cold night he insisted on sitting in the open-air market, in spite of people trying to take him to a hostel. He later collapsed and died of hypothermia.

'R', 'B', and the young woman described in the Introduction, are typical of the alcohol and drug abusers I and others encountered.[5] The key factors were not the immediate symptom, but what had brought those about – the isolation from the mainstream of society, not belonging anywhere and, if they once had, having been rejected.[6] While we speak loosely about the 'option for the poor', the term 'poor' may include not simply the materially poor, but the 'outcast', who lacks social links.[7] It is the latter with whom I am concerned.

This is not to suggest that every person addicted to drink or drugs would answer such a description. There are business and professional people who have taken to drink under pressure of work, or teenagers who have experimented with drugs, and then found themselves addicted. Once their dependency upon drink or drugs has been cured, they have had a supportive family and community to whom they can return. But, as indicated in the Introduction, my concern was with those at the other end of the spectrum.

An essential part of their isolation is that they are seen as a threat to the community because their way of life, albeit not usually undertaken from choice, is different. More will be said about this threat from people on the margins of society in Chapter IV, but the reaction of others, not least those in the Churches, is significant.

I am not entirely unsympathetic towards such a reaction; I can recall my own feelings when I first visited a project for the homeless, long before I was involved in this work. It was Christmas, and I had been invited to spend the day with people who were having a large Christmas dinner for single people, including residents at that project. I felt torn apart; in my head I knew that Jesus would have been with those who felt left out in the cold, but my gut feeling was one of discomfort. It was only later, when I had the opportunity to spend time alongside, and listening to, people whom I might otherwise have regarded as a threat myself, that friendships were able to develop.

Substance abuse and emotional deprivation

Before I set up the Birmingham project I did some research to see what the specialists had to say about the causes of alcohol and drug abuse. A study by the Royal College of Psychiatrists into alcoholism confirmed my observations.[8]

Their findings of a survey into Skid Row drinkers in London would describe most hostels and day centres anywhere. This showed that 58% had experienced parental separation in childhood and the description of the typical Skid Row drinker could have been 'B'. The explanations, such as defect in self-esteem, echo comments above. But of particular interest is the view that drinking may be a purposeful act of 'chronic suicide'.

This 'chronic suicide' explanation would describe 'R' and 'B', and is one which I see in others. For example, there was a man sleeping rough who was admitted to hospital with an abscess on the lung. He spent a while in intensive therapy and then was on an ordinary ward for long enough for the physical dependence on alcohol to disappear. He was found a place in a small, homely hostel, yet he refused to remain there or to attend hospital for follow-up treatment. He stated that he had lived on the streets and wanted to die on the streets – and that is what happened. Another man, in his late sixties and also a heavy drinker, is currently refusing hospital treatment or other help for problems resulting from sleeping rough in sub-zero temperatures.

The self-destruction was apparent with the former, but he said too little about himself for me to know the reason. With the latter the problem is caused by a situation with which he cannot come to terms; drink is a way of deadening the pain temporarily and it is not hard to see his lifestyle on the streets as being suicidal. While writing this, I had a conversation with a drinker in which he was trying to convince me there was nothing that could be done about his drinking. When I queried this, he responded 'I want to die'.

If one accepts that substance abuse may be a form of suicide, then it follows that the form that takes may vary according to circumstances. The three 'stories' I have given, particularly the woman with drug and alcohol abuse, anorexia and depression, illustrate this. Kenneth Leech suggests that such people have always existed, but in times when drugs were not available they might have found some other refuge from their pain.[9] He also quotes the findings of a survey undertaken by the Medical Officer at Holloway Prison which confirm a link between broken homes, emotional disturbance and substance abuse.[10]

Rehabilitation facilities

What was surprising was that many rehabilitation facilities did not take the underlying situation sufficiently into account; the emphasis was on the symptom more than on the causes. Repeatedly I saw people go into residential rehabilitation projects, come out looking healthy and determined to keep their new-found freedom from drink or drugs. However, within weeks, certainly months, despondency and loneliness resulted in a return to substance abuse. One 'dry house' with which I had contact could count its successes over a ten year period on the fingers of one hand.

The people who did manage to get away from their drink or drug dependency tended, as explained above, to be those who had family support, and possibly jobs, to return to, such as the alcoholic businessman or the teenager from an otherwise stable background who experimented with drugs then found him/herself 'hooked'.

Many of the rehabilitation agencies I visited expressed a preference for this 'client group', since work with them was clearly more cost-effective. This being a criterion for the allocation of resources, the better the prognosis, the better are the resources to meet the particular 'problem'. Such agencies therefore depend on the existence of family/ community support for success in overcoming the problem of alcohol/drug abuse.

But there are people for whom the lack of such support is *the* problem. To address the overt problem without the underlying causes may result only in short-term freedom from drugs and alcohol, and then a return to the streets. This may, in my opinion, add to the feeling of being a 'no-hoper' that is common to most people on the streets. I often meet people who have done the rounds of rehabilitation facilities and, having failed so often, have lost the motivation to try again.

Reactions to the problem-centred approach

Meeting this need for affirming, supportive relationships calls for an examination of the role professionals play in the rehabilitation of alcohol/drug abusers. In a setting where professional meets client for the purpose of discussing a specific problem there is a distinction between the professional, who has a body of knowledge and experience, and the client who needs to draw on such skills to solve a problem.

There is indeed a role for the professional, whether it be to discuss a legal problem with a solicitor, or, for example, the possibility of fostering or adopting a child with a social worker. But when there is a need, not only to solve a problem, but to establish relationships which will compensate for the lack of affirmation, particularly in childhood, this distance between professional and client in professional, problem-centred agencies is not the same as a relationship engaging the whole person. Indeed, the very setting in which such contact takes place emphasises the distance, with one sitting behind a desk, often surrounded by the trappings of status and power.

'I am too qualified to do that' is a comment I have heard among social workers anxious to establish that their role is that of a professional, not someone doing the more mundane tasks. Yet Jesus was not too qualified to touch lepers. There must be this willingness to 'touch' people if those in pain are to be reached.

In a Christian context we cannot keep our social relationships totally distinct from relationships with those for whom we are caring. Indeed, there is a contradiction with the incarnational emphasis of an 'apostolic' work if we do. If this relationship of sharing and communion with one another is to be a reality, it requires a reappraisal of the way in which we meet people, whether in pastoral or other professional settings.

I came across other spheres of 'caring' in which this was recognised. For example, facilitating relationships to compensate for earlier lack of affirmation can, in many cases, be more effective than conventional psychotherapy. In *Healing the Unaffirmed: Recognizing Deprivation Neurosis,* Conrad Baars and Anna Terruwe express the view that conventional psychotherapy, which seeks to identify repressed material, does not work for everybody. Their view is that this is because there is no specific 'problem' area that can be pin-pointed and treated; the difficulty lies in lack of affirming relationships starting in childhood which they describe as 'deprivation neurosis'. In some instances they placed patients in what amounted to foster homes where such relationships could develop.[11]

The Samaritans have also recognised the need to address the whole person, not just the problem. When Dr Chad Varah first set up his service to the depressed and suicidal, he had a team of volunteers who made tea for those who were waiting to see him. He found that by the time callers saw him, the despondency that had brought them had lifted. It became apparent that contact with these non-professional helpers was at least as valuable as what he was doing; many who came had as much need to be treated as people of worth as to discuss particular problems. Hence the growth of a service which consisted for the most part of people who were befrienders as opposed to professional counsellors.[12]

I can relate to the effectiveness of this approach in my personal experience. I had been subjected to a degrading form of attack, following which I was put in contact with specialist counsellors concerned with rape and other indecent attacks on women. I was already feeling degraded and humiliated, and the counsellors' emphasis on the details of what had taken place added to that; what I longed for was contact with someone who would help me feel like a normal human being again, instead of seeming to keep me at arms length as a client. I rang the Samaritans and said 'I need a darn good laugh'; when the person answering had recovered from this unusual approach, she pointed out that they were 'open for business' and suggested I went there for a good laugh. Having a pleasant evening, and being accepted as a worthwhile person was a landmark on my journey to recovery.

A key skill in social work and counselling is listening. Listening is, I believe, part of what should take place in normal relationships. There are indeed situations where there are deep-seated emotional problems when skilled help is needed to hear and interpret the underlying statements the other is making, but, with such exceptions, listening and befriending are skills which belong within the Christian community. The very act of listening attentively makes the vital statement that the person being listened to is valued. It is noticeable in many conversations how often people come with their own agendas rather than the desire to hear others and celebrate their worth.

There used to be a story circulating around Oxford about a don who was a great talker and would grasp the buttons on another person's coat as he talked. On one occasion his victim quietly cut the button off and left the room for a while; when he returned the don was still holding the floor – and his coat button.

If there are many people with such poor listening skills as that, doubtless legendary, don, it is not surprising that listening has been appropriated as a professional skill. However, I would strongly agree with Kenneth Leech's view that to institutionalise care into a bureaucratic nine to five pattern is to undermine 'that basic human love which is central to the Christian tradition'.[13] I find that many people in Churches, and doubtless elsewhere, undervalue their own potential to relate to anyone in difficulty, thinking that only someone with specialist training can do so.

Leech attributes this distance, when Church organisations take on what he describes as the 'liberal professional' approach to a desire for tidiness and a kind of purity, a revulsion against mess which dominates so much religious life.

Another approach which keeps its distance is what he calls the 'crusading' approach. This is the person or group who keeps their distance by rushing in to preach, distribute tracts or whatever, to draw people away from the scene. They never stay to listen, get to know people, learn of their feelings, hopes, fears, desires, joys. By their aggressive, insensitive approach to people who are already suffering, they harm both their 'victims' and the credibility of the Christian Church.[14] While this 'crusading' approach may differ in some respects from the 'liberal professional' approach it, too, fails to affirm the person, seeing him/her as a 'case' with a problem – in this instance the need to be brought into Church.

I found similar problems with the 'crusading' approach. In the Introduction I mentioned the young people who needed a base when difficulties arose; they had usually been homeless, sometimes had drug problems, and had been involved in prostitution to support drug habits. The experiences the girls had at a Church I was attending illustrate the point Leech makes about the dangers of the crusading approach; the Church people were anxious to get them into Church – but kept their distance once they were there, with the result that they experienced further rejection.[15]

I encountered this reluctance to relate to people who were 'different' in places where I would not have expected it. Before I started the Birmingham project, I had belonged to a lay Christian organisation which had a commitment to helping the poor. We were working in one of the most deprived parts of Birmingham and were looking around to see what else we might be doing. The group was made up of women only, and as it was an area in which there were many women alcoholics spending much of their time alone in pubs, I suggested that we might spend some of our evenings circulating around pubs in order to get to know them.

'Oh, I don't think those are the sort of people we would want to get involved with', was the response, said with a shudder of revulsion.

I could quote a number of similar situations in which either the status of the professional approach, or the desire for purity, created barriers. If I was conscious of this, there was also the question as to how it appeared to those on the receiving end. The words of Jean Vanier sum this up:

Do not be surprised at rejection by broken people.
They have suffered a great deal
at the hands
of the knowledgeable and the powerful –
doctors, psychologists, sociologists, social workers,
politicians, the police and others.

Rejected people are sick and tired
of 'good' and 'generous' people,
of people who claim to be Christians,
of people who come to them
on their pedestals of pride and power
to do them good.

No wonder their hearts are closed to new people.
They are waiting
for someone who really cares
and who sees in them the light of love and wisdom,
who recognizes their gifts and their beauty;
someone who will accept them just as they are
with no preconceived ideas
that they should change.
They are waiting
for someone who accepts their need to be changed,
one who is willing to know the pain of growth
and who can become vulnerable enough to love,
and so discover the pearl of great price.[16]

This indeed calls for a willingness to enter the situation of the marginal person, to leave behind the trappings of status and power, and put oneself into a position to receive.

A further difficulty in bridging this communication gap is that marginal people, such as those discussed, fall outside the sphere of professional agencies. Those involved with social work and counselling are primarily concerned with people who are an integral part of society; they presuppose that a link exists, that there is a single problem and that, when resolved, the person is able to function within, and be supported by, society again. Such agencies are therefore part of the dominant social structure enabling that structure, and those within it, to function according to its norms. It is not their role to question the underlying causes of such problems, and whether the structure itself might be at fault.

Street people, on the other hand, do not belong within the mainstream of society, and lack the normal social and economic links with it. Their 'problem' is the lack of such links, rather than the symptoms of this alienation.

Throughout scripture there is emphasis on the need to care for the 'stranger', with the exhortation 'remember you were strangers in the land of Egypt'[17] highlighting the solidarity with the marginal person that was expected of God's people. This finds its climax in Jesus' outline of his own ministry: 'I have come to bring good news for the poor . . . '[18] Yet in practice people in the Churches see their role in a very different way. Either they adopt the methodology of secular problem-centred social work, or their approach keeps its distance in other ways.

We need to look at the experience of those who have attempted to bridge this gap, and how the Churches responded once such people themselves moved into the margins of society to meet those there.

II. A Clash of Cultures

It is one thing to say that we need to meet people where they are at, but another matter to bridge that gap in practice. A situation which occurred while I was working at a short-stay hostel for girls – I was doing my social work training with an agency concerned with homeless young people – was a milestone in recognising the nature of the difficulty.

A girl was brought in – I use the term 'brought in' deliberately because she had difficulty walking unaided. She was a drug abuser who had recently spent a short time in hospital following an overdose; from this she went on to a bad acid (LSD) trip on top of large quantities of speed (amphetamines). While she did not need further hospital treatment, no hostel would accept her in that condition, and the one where I was working was full to overflowing.

I had two options. Either I could take her home with me, or she would have to go back to the streets where her prospects while she was in that condition were not promising. She therefore came home with me, as others who had needed a non-institutional base had done. I was anxious as to how I would cope, so another girl who had stayed with me, and who had years of personal experience of the drug scene, offered to join us later.

No sooner had we got home than there was a knock on the door; it was someone from the Church I was attending. Thinking this was heaven-sent help, I welcomed him in; he took one look at the girl, said he was not stopping but had just called in to leave a book. On the way out he muttered to me as he passed 'rather you than me'. This was further evidence of the way people in the streets and those in the Churches felt ill at ease with one another. Later that night the girl who had offered to help turned up – as high as a kite and accompanied by a drug pusher. Far from help having arrived at last, it could be said that the last state was worse than the first.

I could not see how I could be obedient to the gospel and pass by on the other side when I encountered people in such a situation. Yet on my own I was clearly in a difficult position; this was the case not only in such an extreme situation as that above, but being alone with disturbed young people can be a strain at the best of times as anyone who has worked in residential care knows well. In some cases it can also be dangerous.

I had for some years acted as a substitute family to a number of people, such as those already described, who had no family. Any young person leaving home needs somewhere to which they can return, particularly when problems arise; for the people whom I met there was no such place, although they were more vulnerable than most. Then there were the people who had had alcohol or drug problems. They needed people who were there for them when they felt 'down'; most people need the company of others when times are difficult, and those who have had the kind of start in life such as I have described need somewhere where they can feel accepted as they are, 'warts and all'.

I compared my situation with that of residential care workers, since I found myself crumbling under the pressure, while they survived albeit with difficulty. I realised that they had a support system, colleagues who stood in for them during their off-duty times, and their own space to which they could retreat.

Personally, I would suggest that anyone considering sharing their home with a young adult or other adult such as those I have described should bear in mind that if it does not work out, the resulting rejection can add to the existing sense of rejection from past family difficulties. I have sometimes had people coming to me, either guilt-ridden because they have tried to share their home with someone and it has not worked out, or because they feel they ought to do so but are wondering how they would cope. If it is a family who are considering taking such a step, there is the added difficulty that the person to whom hospitality is being given can play one family member off against another – as can happen in any family.

My usual advice is not to rush into any home-sharing arrangement; even when there are no added stresses, as people who have shared flats with friends will know, it can test even the best of relationships to the limit. A potential solution is to do everything one can to ensure that the person has somewhere suitable to stay within reach, and then to offer them hospitality for meals, for coffee, and in general to provide them with a 'home from home'. Preferably more than one household should be involved in this.

This points to a responsibility on the part of the Christian community as a whole, not least because of the emphasis on caring for people such as the 'orphan' and the 'stranger', which occurs frequently in scripture. It calls for an apostolic approach; entering no man's land, and being present to people where they are at. Yet, a gulf between the Churches and those on the streets was apparent; the Birmingham project attempted to bridge this gulf.

It was intended to be a response to the social needs of people on the streets. What was significant in the treatment of alcohol and drug abusers was the link between social relationships and successful rehabilitation; the better the support, the better the prognosis. It was also intended to be part of the move into the 'global' stage of the Church, as outlined in the Introduction, by being a Christian presence on the streets, to involve people from the Churches and so address the difficulty street people experience relating to them and *vice versa*, by meeting people where they were.

It was prompted on the one hand by my own experience, and on the other hand by the experience of others. I had spent time working in New York for Teen Challenge, a Church-based agency whose concerns included drug abusers – mostly from a background similar to the people with whom I was concerned.

A follow-up study of people who had been through their rehabilitation programme demonstrated that success was related to incorporation into a caring community, such as a Church. Where recovering addicts had been unable to relate to a Church, it was found that each had been uncomfortable with those from a different background. This had led to the recognition that there were lessons to be learned from the approach to Third World communities; each needed to be met where they were, and communicated with in ways which were culturally relevant.

I took the Incarnation as the model for this Christian presence, in contrast to the problem-centred approach of conventional social work. I began to live in a deprived inner-city area in order to be within reach of the places where street people congregate. I felt this might go some way towards breaking down the barrier between 'worker' and 'client'; not only was there the availability, but the living situation also brought me nearer to the lifestyle of the inner city. For these reasons it seemed more appropriate to describe it as an 'apostolic' work instead of as a social work project.

The views of members of the local Church were expressed by a petition to bring the project to an end, accompanied by threats to leave the Church if this was not done. A meeting with all petitioners, at which a bishop was present to support the project, was required to reassure them that the work would not be undertaken in a way that would cause problems in the neighbourhood.

One outcome of this meeting was support from outside the local Church. Once the reassurance as to the way the project was to operate had been given, support came from those who had their own experience of marginality. While little support was forthcoming from the local Church, there were those from Churches elsewhere who responded to the request for involvement in the work.

The aim was not so much to provide additional practical services as to 'be present' to people where they were, in a supportive, befriending role. The main problem in rehabilitating people with drug and alcohol problems was the long-term support in the community, where there were few existing links with the family or community. Therefore my initial intention was to build links with hostels and rehabilitation facilities, get to know residents, so that when they were ready to move on, they would not be as isolated as previously.

However, one cannot impose relationships on people; they have to grow, with each side having the freedom to choose whether that relationship continues, or not.

Street people are used to relating to professionals, and possibly also to volunteers who are acting in a supporting role. But while such contacts can have their place, there is an element of 'us' and 'them'; one is in a position of power that can emphasise the powerlessness of the other. The passage from Jean Vanier, quoted in the previous chapter, shows great insight into reactions to such relationships, and the kind of contact they are looking for.

Most friendships have their origin in shared interests, so an important question was, how relationships between people from different backgrounds could be built up. Sport and other recreational activities span social barriers; therefore the plan was to bring people from the Churches together with those in the hostels through sharing such activities. In one town a Church group, consisting of middle-aged men and their sons, in their late teens and early twenties, got to know young people in a night shelter through playing football with them. Football led to evenings playing board games in the night shelter; it was a natural progression for them to want to remain in contact with one another when residents were rehoused.

However, this was an exception. Many volunteers were prepared to undertake tasks, such as helping with the soup kitchens which were another aspect of the project, where there was the security of a clear-cut role of giving practical help. Most were not prepared to move on to activities that involved building relationships of mutual friendship.

Arising from the soup kitchens, a few of us used to meet six homeless men to have supper together once a week, while others ate with some young people living in a 'squat'. But less than ten percent of the volunteers responded. With the exception of one person, all these came from the same Church, one that was going through a period of growing awareness of the situation of people on the fringes of society.

Among this minority of volunteers, there were a number

of comments about what they had gained from meeting those on the streets, and in particular seeing how they handled existence without the possessions and status that others take for granted.

The majority of those encountered led an individualistic lifestyle. Some were literally homeless, sleeping in derelict buildings, deliberately not advertising their whereabouts in order not to attract attention which might have resulted in police action to move them on. There was also an element of mutual suspicion; while they associated with others at a superficial level they were not prepared to share the little privacy they had in their 'skippers' – the term used for the derelict buildings in which they slept.

There were others, who had been rehoused following a period on the streets but who had problems both with the isolation of their flats and the financial difficulties of living on state benefits. Whether state benefits are adequate for day-to-day living expenses is debatable; the problem increases with time as additional expenses, such as replacing shoes and other clothing, arise. Hence many continued to spend time at day centres and soup kitchens both for the company and for material help.

Others, particularly groups of younger people, adopted a semi-communal lifestyle which in some instances resembled that of the hippies of the sixties. While these were a minority, there were elements of a 'counter-culture' which included protest against what its members saw as the causes of their situation.

Of particular interest was the attitude to relationships and possessions. The young people living in the 'squat' shared their vision of a society based on sharing belongings and relating on the basis of the worth of each individual, not on domination of one by another. After one such evening I was reading the following words by Leonardo Boff:

The meaning of human life is not found in creating riches, but fraternity; it is supported not by having, but by being one with – and compassionate – with all creatures.[19]

This encapsulated so well what the young people had been

saying that I pinned it up on the walls of my living room and awaited their reaction the following week. I neither commented nor drew their attention to it but, when they spotted it, it was clear that it said it all.

The majority of volunteers, however, while conscientiously providing practical help, kept their distance. This gap between the people in the Churches and those on the streets has been a feature of a number of projects and was the reason why the Salvation Army came into existence.

William Booth had not set out with the intention of founding an organisation outside the existing Churches, but once he began working with people on the streets he found that the two did not mix. According to one account he

> deeply offended the respectable members of the Wesleyan Chapel which he attended by invading their comfortable sanctimony with a crowd of roughs from the slums of Nottingham whom he marched into the chapel on a Sunday and placed in conspicuous pews. The deacons, whose noses had been offended as deeply as their sense of decorum, rebuked the young enthusiast, who declined to promise not to bring his band of roughs into select company again and would agree only to pass them through the back door and to seat them in less conspicuous pews.[20]

I might have been less surprised at my own experiences had I been aware at the time that no less a person than William Booth had had an even harder time with his co-religionists.

More recently, a mission was held in a Birmingham parish which included at one end a run-down council estate, and at the other end middle-class owner-occupied housing. The Church building was in the latter area, and the big problem was drawing in people from the housing estate, but the mission had made some headway. When the missioner did a follow-up visit, one of the middle-class regular parishioners told him 'We've managed to get rid of those dreadful people who started coming to Church after your mission'.

Nor is this discomfort one-sided, as I have recently been reminded. A well-known, popular man who had been sleeping rough in Birmingham for over twenty years recently died.

Although all the major decisions for the funeral were made by his friends, when the time came I noticed some of them missing. I found that they had been too embarrassed to come because they did not have smart clothes. The congregation was made up of people who, if not literally homeless, were unemployed and poor themselves. But those who came wore dark jackets and ties. Those who did not have what were seen as the right clothes stayed away. It was impossible to persuade them that 'Church' was not concerned with outward appearances of respectability. Many, who have worked among those who do not relate to the middle-class culture which characterises most Churches, have experienced similar difficulty.

William Booth's description of his experience is, in effect, a framework for any outreach to those who do not relate to that dominant culture:

My first idea was simply to get the people saved and send them to the Churches. This proved at the outset impracticable.

First, they would not go when sent.

Second, they were not wanted.

And third, we wanted some of them at least ourselves to help us in the business of saving others.

We were thus driven to providing for the converts ourselves.[21]

He therefore reached people through open-air services, and provided for his converts through what later became known as the 'corps', the congregations of Salvationists.

Not only did his converts not relate to established congregations, but Booth himself had difficulty relating to existing Churches.

He was for some time a Wesleyan local preacher. When he resigned in order to preach in the open air, he found his membership had been withheld. He encountered similar difficulties with the New Connection, a branch of Methodism. The Church tried to get him to abandon his special mission in favour of regular ministry 'ostensibly for reasons of the red-tape order, probably due in reality to promptings of jealousy'.[22] When he requested reappointment as an Evangelist, W. T.

Stead describes the scenes in the conference hall as a 'useful reminder of the blindness and folly which almost every ecclesiastical assembly appears to have inherited from the Sanhedrin'.[23]

The above suggests that Booth himself, not only those who were outside the dominant culture, was seen as a threat. In Chapter IV it will be suggested that it may not only be individuals *per se* who are seen as a threat, but also the *state* of marginality. Those who voluntarily enter that state may themselves be contaminated by it.

There are other situations when leaders find it necessary to pioneer their own methodology. As a result, they come into conflict with the established Churches. It is often difficult to pin-point the reason for such conflict, though its prevalence suggests that an element of 'threat' from the margins may be there.

Other projects have produced fewer written accounts of their work than the Salvation Army or Teen Challenge. From the material available it is, however, possible to see similarities and differences. What is of interest is to see the way in which the projects and individuals vary as to the extent to which they enter into dialogue, as opposed to one-way communication, with those among whom they worked.

Anfield Road Fellowship in Liverpool found that traditional Church structures entailed a financial commitment which left a local Church burdened with maintenance of buildings and full-time clergy. This placed constraints on it when it wished to give priority to people who did not have the financial resources to support a conventional Church. They therefore met in an ordinary house and the leader, Dave Cave, and his wife became self-supporting.

The first members came from Dave's previous Church where they were 'struggling with traditional Church spirituality'. After initial suspicion other Churches discovered that the Fellowship was reaching the kind of people they could not reach. The clue to this lay in the question of how people were trained for leadership. It was recognised that conventional training resulted in people losing their class base and local accents, sounding like outsiders and hence being less able to reach the local people.[24]

This echoes discussions which took place in both the Salvation Army and Teen Challenge. The early Salvationists realised that conventional training for ministry could take people away from their social origins into a middle-class milieu, and so reduce their ability to communicate with people from a working-class background. They, therefore, set up their own training school, specifically geared towards training for the kind of ministry the Salvation Army was undertaking. A similar debate took place at Teen Challenge, with no awareness that the Salvationists had faced the same question and reached the same conclusion a hundred years earlier.

The fellowship saw its task as to become the 'grit in the oyster'. The grit in an oyster's shell causes aggravation, inflammation and irritation, but can eventually produce a pearl. The fellowship was to have such an effect; while in some ways it might be an irritant to the Church, the ultimate intention was that of producing 'the pearl of great price'.[25]

The chapter on the Hope Community from Margaret Hebbelthwaite's *Basic is Beautiful* contains no such explicit references to relationships with Churches. However, its very existence was the result of the local Roman Catholic parish priest's reluctance to become involved with the poor housing estate in which the community was set up, in spite of it being within his parish.[26]

Sister Margaret, of the Hope Community, quotes from an unknown author:

Our first task in approaching another culture, another religion, is to take off our shoes, for the place we are approaching is holy. Else we may forget that God was there before we arrived.[27]

Significantly, she says that she had been more evangelised by the people among whom she was working than she had been evangelised. For this reason, she felt that by listening to and learning from them, and by responding creatively to meet their needs, the whole Church could be renewed. People on the estate where the community was established were seen to be freer to explore new models of Church and of liturgy, since they were not bound by norms and conventions which others might find hard to abandon after years of practice.[28]

This question of being evangelised by those among whom an 'apostolic' work is established can be seen in the work of Sister Eileen Carroll, a religious sister, who works among the homeless in Leeds and takes Vincent Donovan's experience with the Masai in East Africa, as described in *Christianity Rediscovered* as her model. She found that in Donovan's description of the need for a distinctive approach to the Masai, she could substitute 'homeless' for 'Masai'. In one newsletter she quotes Donovan's view of evangelisation:

a) Evangelisation is a process of bringing the gospel to people where they are, not where you would like them to be.

b) Do not try to call people back to where they were, and do not try to call them to where you are, beautiful as that place might seem to you. You must have the courage to go with them to a place that neither you nor they have ever been before.[29]

She refers to the need for a 'change of heart' but that that did not have to take place only in the person who was homeless and alcoholic, but 'also in the hearts of the rest of us'. One of the stated aims of a group, consisting of people from the Churches who met regularly for a social evening with street people, was 'We hope to keep on *being changed* ourselves. . . .'

To summarise, the findings of all the agencies discussed demonstrate the distinction between the social milieu of those in the Churches and those on the streets. Following from this is the recognition, explicit or implicit, of a parallel with the Third World. In each instance there is the attempt to build a community which takes into account the social situation of the people concerned.

However, a distinction can be seen when one asks whether the communication is one-way or two-way. Does the Church, or Church-based agency, set out with a 'message' it needs to convey, or does it go in in order to build community with the people concerned?

Evangelical Churches, or agencies, such as the Salvation Army or Teen Challenge, would be mainly concerned with conveying a message. Where they are engaged in rehabilitating those with alcohol and drug problems, conversion will be seen as an important stage in the struggle to be free from addiction; this model has been adopted by a number of Church-based drug rehabilitation projects such as New Life Foundation, Life for the World, Coke Hole Trust, and Yeldall Manor. There are those who might not agree with their theological stance, and particularly their emphasis on conversion. The validity of their rehabilitation model is, however, borne out by its similarity to the Twelve Steps of Alcoholics Anonymous, which have been used to meet the needs of other groups such as Narcotics Anonymous and Gamblers Anonymous. The Steps are reproduced as an appendix. The way AA stresses the need to admit powerlessness over alcohol, to surrender the will to God, as he is understood, is paralleled by the conversion experience. Although not explicitly stated in the Twelve Steps, AA encourages ongoing membership of the 'fellowship', i.e. of AA, which reflects the need for a supportive community.

The 'conversion experience' is not only comparable to the Twelve Steps of AA; it also relates to the *metanoia* of traditional Christian spirituality. It cannot be disputed that change and growth is a biblical principle, but the question is what the individual is changing from. If, as has been suggested, the person's problem is linked with low self-esteem then there is the need for a spirituality which affirms and redresses the causes. The basis for self-esteem is that human nature was given incomparable dignity through the Incarnation; whatever failings have contributed to the human situation they do not alter that crucial fact.

The value of the AA model, and those which can be seen to follow a similar pattern, can be appreciated. However, there is a question mark as to how an approach which emphasises the part played by the individual's sin in his/her situation relates to this need for affirmation. In some instances, such approaches can put the entire responsibility for what has gone wrong on the individual concerned, without looking at the pressures on those individuals as to how they exercise their free will.

An examination of the situation of the immediate families, and their relationship to the wider social, economic and political structures, might have suggested that the individual can only be seen in that context, and that there are factors there which need to be redressed. The lack of evidence of factors in the wider society being questioned may be linked to the post-Constantine relationship to secular structures when the Churches were less inclined to challenge flaws in society. It may also, in the case of the agencies in question, be linked to a view of poverty being mainly the responsibility of the poor themselves. E. P. Thompson gives a graphic description of such a view:

> with its denunciation of sloth and improvidence in the labourer, and its convenient belief that – if success was a sign of election – poverty was itself evidence of spiritual turpitude.[30]

On the other hand there are those attempting to listen to the underlying factors in society, and so build a community which seeks to redress those factors. This is where the lifestyle of the counter cultures is significant; it is a more explicit statement as to how they perceive their situation and its causes than the relatively passive response of those following a more individualistic lifestyle.

Then there is the conflict which becomes apparent when such attempts to bring those on the streets together with those in the Churches are made. There are those who see not only the street people but those who work with them as a threat – in the same that General Booth was regarded with suspicion. Others who have overcome this barrier have found they have been the ones to gain from entering into a relationship. This, together with the statements being made by the counter cultures, raises the question of the theological response in general and the significance of marginality in the life of the Churches in particular.

III. God in the Cultural Melting Pot

A parallel between St Paul's experience with the Jerusalem Church and William Booth's repeated difficulties with the Church to which he belonged, may not at first be obvious. Yet the difficulty experienced by several of the projects discussed in the last chapter suggests that a transition not unlike that experienced by the early Church when it moved from its Jewish roots into the Gentile world may need to take place.

In each instance there is a conflict between what is culturally important to the respective groups and what is essential to the gospel. In one, there is the attempt by the Jewish Christians to impose the full range of Jewish customs and laws on Gentile converts. In the other the conflict is between different social classes and their lifestyles, with each feeling uncomfortable with the other.

'Church? That's all posh 'ats and tea parties,' a Cockney lady once commented to me; however exaggerated her view of Church it did illustrate that she perceived it to be linked with an alien lifestyle. There is therefore a need to distinguish between what is the 'good news' for the community concerned, and what is cultural 'baggage' which they do not need to take on board.

The new set of questions to be addressed as the Churches move into the third, global stage fall into two broad categories, and the theologies which emerge reflect this. Robert Schreiter speaks of the 'liberation' model, which seeks to redress factors which may be at the root of deprivation or injustice, and the 'ethnographic', concerned with entering into dialogue with the culture of the community in question.[31]

This distinction is helpful in that, on surveying various contemporary theologies, there do appear to be these two elements. They have either looked for biblical answers to questions such as racial, political or economic exploitation, or social deprivation affecting that particular community as a whole, and/or they have sought to express Christian faith in terms that are culturally relevant to that community.

The 'liberation' model

Schreiter's liberation model is relevant to the situation of the more visible street people, i.e. the drifting individuals who are outside any structure, when considering the reasons why they are there, and what should be the Churches' response.

Political and economic factors have a part in the situation of street people. But specific to that situation is their alienation from the mainstream of society and the resulting low self-esteem, often related to substance abuse. This link raises the question as to what role the Churches play in providing affirmation through their spirituality and the quality of relationships within the Church community.

At the time I first researched this question in the mid 1980s a high percentage of those on the streets were of Roman Catholic origin. The figures given in the report *Alcohol and Alcoholism*[32] correlate with my own findings.

A survey of Skid Row drinkers showed 37% to be Irish and 27% Scots. Most of the former and a substantial percentage of the latter are likely to have had a Roman Catholic background. The overall figures obtained from hostels indicated that around 50% gave their religion as Roman Catholic, and were of Irish or Scots origins. During the week towards the end of 1985 when these figures were being collected, the Salvation Army hostel in Birmingham had recorded 60% of their residents as being of Roman Catholic origin, with an estimate that the overall figure for Salvation Army hostels throughout the country was 50%.

The age range within which alcohol abuse was found was the 30+ age range, with the more chronic abusers in an older age group. Since that time there has been an increase in the number of younger alcohol abusers, and people who combine alcohol with other drugs.

From the above it could be deduced that a high proportion of the middle aged people on the streets have been influenced by the kind of spirituality which was common in the Roman Catholic Church before the influence of the Second Vatican Council was felt. A number of comments have been made by street people brought up in Roman Catholic orphanages and/or educated in Roman Catholic schools. These indicated more emphasis on the sinfulness of the individual than on his or her unique worth in the sight of God, which appeared to have contributed to their low self-esteem. Such views are confirmed by the writings of others, such as Baars and Terruwe, and Hughes, which will be discussed below, suggesting that it is a trait which cannot be ignored.

It is unlikely that Roman Catholics are alone in this. It is likely that the same problem might be encountered among people who had experienced a combination of lack of childhood affirmation and a religious upbringing that stressed the total depravity of human nature, as do some Protestant denominations. The remarks that follow could therefore be equally applied to others, but because these reflections arise from work within a Roman Catholic setting more specific reference is made to such a background.

It is likely that there has been a change in the composition of the various groups one encounters on the streets since I undertook this research, with a lower proportion coming from Roman Catholic backgrounds. However, if the Christian community as a whole is to seek dialogue with those who have 'dropped out' of the mainstream of society, it is relevant to examine the factors which contribute to, or detract from, affirmation and emotional well-being in Christian spirituality in general.

This question of affirmation, including its relevance to the Roman Catholic situation, is picked up by Conrad Baars and Anna Terruwe in *Healing the Unaffirmed: Recognising Deprivation Neurosis.*

In their view the main problem with a number of people is arrested emotional development. This is caused by a lack of affirming relationships present in normal family life which form part of emotional growth, hence the term 'deprivation neurosis'. More traditional psychiatry looks for identifiable emotional illness, such as the neuroses normally treated by the recognition of repressed emotions through psychotherapy. In their opinion such a probing for repressed traumas or emotions can be counter-productive when there is the more general problem of a lack of normal emotional development. When a child's essential need for loving acceptance has been frustrated, his emotional growth comes to a standstill, resulting in clinical symptoms.

They devote a chapter to case histories where existing treatment had failed, but where symptoms are relieved by recognition of, and treatment for, such emotional deprivation.

They describe how religious faith, if there has been any, has also been arrested since emotional development has not kept pace with intellectual development. Faith tends to be revived if, and only if, religion comes to be seen as the experiencing of love of, and for, God. Like anyone else, these individuals want love not only in their natural lives, but also in their supernatural life with God.

They go on to discuss the more specific problem with the Roman Catholic Church. In particular, it may repel the 'unaffirmed' with its legalism and fear of punishment rather than offering them an affirmation of their whole being. As a result, God is seen as a threatening force, reinforcing their existing low self-esteem.

The following quotation from a letter written by a patient of theirs could have been written by a typical street person, particularly one of Irish Roman Catholic origins:

My inner fear has taken on form from what I heard about God. It was always God who made things wrong, who made it possible to do things wrong. More and more, things were turned into threats by God. My only purpose in life was to keep things right in the eyes of God.[33]

This is similar to the description given by Sister Eileen Carroll in Chapter II relating to the fear of death she encountered among street people.

The remedy is to create an environment for the patient in which affirming relationships can be fostered. This compensates for the earlier lack of affirmation. The significance is that the potential for 'healing' therefore comes not only from the 'professional' but from others around the patient. This has clear implications for the way Churches function in terms of the day-to-day relationships within it; a Church with healthy 'body life' can also be a healing community.

Gerard Hughes illustrates this question of false images of God with his description of children's introduction to 'Uncle George' in *God of Surprises*. 'Uncle George' is a portrayal of God, who is a family member much admired by the parents. The children are told that he is very loving, a great friend of the family who is powerful and interested in all of them. Then comes the great moment when they are taken to visit him. However, it turns out that he lives in a formidable mansion, is bearded, gruff and threatening. The children cannot share their parents' admiration for this prized relation.

At the end of the visit, Uncle George speaks severely to the children, telling them that he expects to see them in his mansion once a week. He emphasises this by telling them what will happen if they do not turn up; there is a graphic description of the fires of hell, with its unearthly screams, into which anyone who fails to visit Uncle George, or act in a way he approves, will be thrown. The imaginary children are then taken back to their parents; as they return home, clutching their parents' hands, Mum says 'And now don't you love Uncle George with all your heart and soul, mind and strength?' The children, in spite of their loathing for him, make out that they agree, fearing that to do otherwise would be to join the queue at the furnace.[34]

This story is set within the context of likening the stages of spiritual growth to human development – infancy, adolescence and adulthood. These correspond with the institutional, critical, and mystical elements in the spiritual life; each need to be present if that life is to be balanced.

There is a parallel between the institutional element in religion, and the 'super-ego' in human development. Overemphasis on the institutional element, particularly if it includes an imposition of moral teaching combined with threats of eternal damnation for non-observance and excludes the critical and mystical, can have the same effect as a harsh super-ego, inhibiting growth to mature adulthood. In the same way as heavy parenting will produce a harsh super-ego, so Christianity imposed in this way will develop a tyrannical religious super-ego, stifling the individual personality, depriving them of inner freedom and leading them into a state of Christian neurosis. This is a reversal of the view of Christ's yoke being easy and light; instead it becomes a painful burden which buries people under its weight of anxiety and guilt.[35]

It is this burden of anxiety and guilt which is potentially damaging for people who already carry too much emotional 'baggage'. The discrepancy, between Christ's description of his yoke as easy and light and the reality of the image of God communicated to many, raises the question as to the reason for the latter. A clue to this can be seen in Elaine Pagels' *Adam, Eve, & the Serpent*, particularly in the chapter 'The Politics of Paradise' in which she outlines contrasting attitudes towards the human situation.

Pagels suggests that most Christians during the first three centuries would have agreed with Gregory of Nyssa's view that God created the world as a royal dwelling place for the human race which was fit to exercise royal rule through being created in the living image of the universal King.[36] By contrast, Augustine considered that the entire human race had inherited from Adam a nature so damaged by sin that even the most tyrannical human government becomes an indispensable defence against the forces sin has let loose in human nature.[37]

Augustine's views won the day. His theory of original sin proved politically expedient, persuading many of his contemporaries that human beings universally need external government – which meant, in their case, both a Christian state and an imperially supported Church. According to Pagels, it also offered an analysis of human nature that became the major influence on their psychological and political thinking of all subsequent generations of western Christians.[38] Whether or not Pagels is right in blaming Augustine, what is significant is the extent to which a pessimistic view of human nature affects images of God, and hence perceptions of the individual's worth.

However, according to Richard McBrien, contemporary theologians 'reject the notion (suggested by Augustine and others) that Original Sin is more pervasive and more universal than is redemption . . . .'[39] Among those contemporary theologians is Karl Rahner who says that

It may be assumed that sin was only permitted by God within the domain of his unconditional and stronger salvific will, which from the very beginning was directed towards God's self-communication in Christ.[40]

The views of those such as Rahner should correct the imbalance to be found in the way Christian teaching is sometimes presented.

It is apparent, particularly from Hughes' account, that some of the images people had of God sharply contrasted with those to be found in the gospel; there would be a contradiction if Christian teaching was found to be counter-productive to emotional wholeness and maturity.

A clear statement from the Jesuits' thirty-fourth General Council is that the Society's mission derives from the continuing experience of the Crucified and Risen Christ who invites people to join him in preparing the world to become the completed Kingdom of God. Part of this is to help people to free themselves from false images they have of themselves in order to discover their true identity as being 'in God's light, completely like Christ'.[41]

There is then the way in which a more positive, affirming, view of human beings might be 'fleshed out'. Baars and Terruwe believe that a remedy for 'deprivation neurosis' must lie in reproducing the conditions under which emotional life can resume its natural growth.[42] This is done, at least in the first stage, through placing patients in a family environment where they will receive the affirmation lacking in their childhood development. Although Baars and Terruwe do not place this treatment within a biblical context, they might well have done so, particularly in the light of the Jesuit statement, which goes to the heart of the gospel to pinpoint the true source of affirmation.

The responsibility to care for orphans is a recurring exhortation, and those who, although not literally orphans, have been deprived of normal family life and relationships could be seen in this light. There has indeed been the provision of children's homes by agencies such as the National Children's Homes, the Children's Society, and the various Roman Catholic diocesan agencies. But in most instances this has not moved on to the incorporation within the Churches of those who are not part of nuclear families.

The day-to-day life and activities of most Churches focuses on the nuclear family. Major celebrations, other than those relating to the various seasons of the Church's year, are mainly those which concern the family, i.e. marriage, baptisms, where infant baptism is practised, or dedications, confirmation and (for some) First Holy Communion. While these may be seen as celebrations for the whole congregation, they do focus on the families concerned, and there is an unspoken assumption that everyone is part of such a nuclear family which is their main source of companionship and fellowship.

There are seldom activities that would bring someone who is not part of such a family into contact with other Church members. The very young and the very old may be catered for through mid-week activities, but not other 'singles', which, as has been indicated, is the situation of most street people.

A Church which is seeking to be relevant to street people therefore needs to be aware of the social and emotional needs of 'singles'. To some extent the lay communities which came into existence as a result of the charismatic movement, particularly in the United States, have taken this into account.

One of the first such communities was that which grew up round the Church of the Redeemer, Houston, Texas. There, families opened their homes to singles who lived as part of an extended family. The Word of God Community, Ann Arbor, Michigan, developed a more flexible structure. While in some instances singles did join families, there were also households of singles. Those who preferred a more independent living situation were either attached to regular households, or formed into 'non-residential households' of people who met together for dinner and socialising at regular times during the week when there were no activities involving the community as a whole.[43]

In such models of 'Church' there is therefore a recognition of the social, as well as spiritual, needs of the single adult. While this may occur on an informal basis in other Churches, there is a likelihood that singles, particularly those from the kind of disrupted family background common to so many street people, may be left on the fringe of the Church.

In a Church with a strong corporate life embracing people of all ages, single as well as married, the individual should be able to discover his or her true identity and worth. A community which recognises the implications of the Incarnation will demonstrate this by the way it values its members.

On this question, of the need for affirmation, the pro-life movement holds a clue which I believe has not been fully exploited. I see it, not as an issue concerned mainly with anti-abortion campaigning, but as one which is central to the Christian gospel in that it concerns the unique value in the sight of God of each human life, regardless of his/her potential in the eyes of society. As such, the pro-life person should have a special concern to address the situation of the marginal person whom society has rejected.

I would like to see the term 'pro-marginal' used in this context instead of 'pro-life'. This would endorse the value of life at every stage, from conception to death, and is in line with the option for the poor. The term 'pro-life' is not only primarily associated with anti-abortion activity, but also, in the context of the United States, is associated with the views of people who, while anti-abortion, do not opt for the poor at subsequent stages in the life cycle.

The approach to all in need should be a pro-life one in its widest sense. Yet, in practice, distinctions are made between the 'deserving' and 'undeserving' poor; the latter being those who, society believes, have brought their situation on themselves.

This distinction produces inconsistencies and so emphasises the need for 'pro-life' thinking to permeate every area. To illustrate this point from the Roman Catholic scene, many people are actively involved in anti-abortion campaigning; they may also in the past have been involved in fund-raising for children in the care of Roman Catholic agencies. A less popular cause would be the homeless alcoholic sitting on a park bench with his meths bottle.

But that homeless alcoholic may well have been the angelic face of a little boy on publicity material for a Roman Catholic agency's fund-raising campaign years before. Many people on the streets began life, or spent part of their childhood, in institutional care. He might also have been the result of an unwanted pregnancy which was continued as a result of a Roman Catholic agency's efforts to give the mother an alternative to termination.

The sense of rejection and low self-worth may have been a key factor leading to alcohol abuse. It could be argued that in taking to drink he exercised his free-will, which was not a factor in his earlier situation, but the pressures on him as to how he exercised that free will are the result of a situation over which he had no control. His worth in the sight of God is not diminished. The pro-life movement does indeed affirm the worth of human life, but if it is to be true to the Incarnation it needs to give that affirmation from conception to death, not only to birth.

The 'ethnographic' model and Minjung theology

A theological model which enters into dialogue with a culture, illustrating Schreiter's ethnographic model, and which speaks both to the 'outcast' in this country and in the Third World, is to be found in Korea. It has arisen from the 'minjung', a word derived from two Chinese characters, *min* (= people) and *jung* (= mass). However, the term does not lend itself to translation, but is defined as 'those who are oppressed politically, exploited economically, alienated sociologically, and kept uneducated in cultural and intellectual matters'.[44]

This needs to be understood within the context of Korean history. There was almost continuous oppression by foreign powers, to which there is no obvious parallel in the West. It goes back so far that the reaction to it is too deeply rooted in the culture to be given any concise definition, such as the occidental mind looks for.

Minjung theology is therefore connected with the 'underdogs' of Korea, and listens to some of the deeper, underlying cultural expressions of such oppression and alienation. The minjung should not be defined because it would make the people an object for study and reflection, according to David Kwang-Sun.[45] This is not fully explained, but taken in context it does suggest the need to be in a position of solidarity with the people concerned, as opposed to relating as a researcher or professional, either of which implies some distance and distinction from the people concerned.

Certain themes emerge which are of particular interest. There is the significance of the use of the term *ochlos*, as opposed to *laos*, for the minjung. When *ochlos* is used in Mark's gospel it is in the context of being oppressed and/or in conflict with the power structure.[46] If the situation of street people is seen as related to issues of powerlessness and marginality, then this is significant in that what emerges from minjung theology has relevance for them.

The concepts of *han* and *dan* describe feelings which could well apply to many on the streets. *Han* is described as 'an underlying feeling of Korean people. On the one hand, it is a dominant feeling of defeat, resignation, and nothingness. On the other, it is a feeling with a tenacity of will for life which comes to weaker beings'. Because of Korea's long history of oppression, the concept of *han* has deep roots in the culture and mythology.[47] *Dan* is 'for the transformation of the secular world and secular attachments. Accumulated *han* being met with continuous *dan*. On the one hand, there is the fearful *han* which can kill, cause revenge, destroy, and hate endlessly, and on the other, there is the repetition of *dan* to suppress the explosion which can break out of the vicious circle, so that *han* can be sublimated as higher spiritual power.'[48]

This acknowledgement of deep-seated feelings has relevance for people whose feelings are expressed, or suppressed, through drugs, alcohol and violence. Does this sublimation of *han* as higher spiritual power bear resemblance to the power coming from the margins described by Mary Douglas, which will be discussed in Chapter IV?

Finally, there is the view that the dignity of all human beings, and hence of the minjung, is related to being made in the image of God.

Human dignity comes from outside the sphere of the human race. The Bible comments not only on human values but also on the meaning of being human. The human race is being created through certain events which occur between God and man. The meaning of being human originates in these events. Therefore, the term "minjung" preserves the full dignity of the human being.[49]

This, again, is significant for the lack of self-esteem to be found among those on the streets. It takes the basis for their self-esteem away from the negative experiences which have undermined it to the relationship with God. The fact that God took human nature, and identified with the outcast, makes a powerful statement about the worth of the individual, particularly those whom others reject.

The overall view of minjung theology is that of sensitivity to the feeling of oppression, and of recognition that the resolution of that must come from within.

The relevance for work with street people is that there is a need to enter the situation in a way that does not demean. Along with this goes a recognition that the end goal of such identification is an empowering of people's own internal resources to counteract those forces which hold them back from fulfilling their human potential.

I was struck, when I was first involved in this area of work, by the untapped potential among those I met. I met highly intelligent people who had left school with nothing to show for it, perhaps because of their social or family situation. For example, one girl with a drug problem had passed the old 'eleven plus' but had not gone to grammar school because her family opposed such a move.

She went to secondary modern school although her performance in IQ tests was better than someone with a recorded IQ of 140. This suggested her intelligence might have been in the Mensa range, yet not only did she have no idea of her own potential, but her low self-esteem underlying her drug abuse included a sense of failure intellectually as well as a general dislike of herself.

I could point to a number of people on the streets who are talented in a variety of ways and, given a different social setting and opportunities, might well have been 'successful' in their chosen fields. Empowerment is therefore a key factor in engagement. It is the pattern of the Incarnation; as Jesus entered the human situation to restore it to its right relationship with God, so we engage with others in order that, together, we might fulfil that human potential.

The final statement of the fifth International Conference of the Ecumenical Association of Third World Theologians includes a passing reference to the internal problems, such as alcoholism, drug abuse, loneliness, suicide, etc., within capitalist countries. This suggests a common link, in terms of being oppressed peoples, between the Third World and street people.

Any parallel between street people and some Third World communities needs qualification. Whereas in the Third World common links and culture are a source of self-esteem to be affirmed, with street people that which they have in common, their rejection by and of mainstream society, is the reverse. However, from a Christian perspective, since Jesus was frequently found with those whom others rejected, their dignity can be seen to derive from the special place they had in His ministry. Similarly, solidarity with them is the place where Christians may discover the Lord's presence.

Active engagement in the lives of such communities is an essential prelude to the 'struggle'. It is pointed out that theologians are not exclusively professional academic theologians. While the latter have an important role in formulating precise and systematic interpretations of different dimensions of the

Christian faith, it is essential that such definitions and the conceptualising process itself are not divorced from the concrete reality of human struggle. Therefore:

other responses to the gospel, such as those of socio-political activists, pastors, social workers, educators, artists, and social scientists, are also considered to fall within the scope of theology.[50]

This reference to the involvement of people from other disciplines opens the door for people to do theology while involved with, as opposed to being distant from, the communities concerned. That action alongside those communities is not only possible, but essential, is also apparent. The prime commitment is to the gospel and faith that the risen Lord is continuing the ministry begun in Galilee. This presents a challenge to discern His presence in the people's struggle and to participate in it ourselves.

One way we can do this is to be open to what is happening in the counter-cultures. Many of the young people I met on the streets identified with the counter-cultures, as described below. As the term suggests, there is a protest against the prevailing culture and the reasons why street people are alienated from it coming from within; the potential for liberation is therefore expressed in the culture itself.

They should be empowered to follow a lifestyle that incorporates their views on relationships with one another and with the created world. Like the han-dan dialectic, this is thus transforming what might have been negative, self-destructive tendencies in the individual, and hence the group, into a constructive way of life which could encourage others to a more creative lifestyle.

The ethnographic model and the Catholic Worker Movement

An aspect of the counter-cultures to be found among the street people who live a communal existence is the interest shown in anarchism. This is clearly a reaction against the nature of the power structures which they regard as contributing to their situation.

Some similarity with the hippies of the 1960s and the New Age Movement can be seen in such groups. I had noticed the tendency of some people to leave the city and join up with New Age travellers; this would be particularly evident at the time of the Glastonbury Festival or the season for harvesting 'magic' mushrooms. According to Sarah Lonsdale this link between young people on the streets and New Age travellers is recognised. In an article in *The Observer* she draws on the views of Professor John Drane of Stirling University who has identified several distinct groups among the traveller fraternity. There are the middle-class dropouts, the descendants of the 1960s hippies, there are the unemployed, people escaping the tax system and the sixteen- and seventeen-year olds, who have been cut out of the benefits system. 'They feel society has turned its back on them, so they turn their backs on society'.[51]

One of the attractions of this lifestyle is the mutual support. One such traveller, in describing their lifestyle, saw that, while the traveller society may be introspective, its members look after one another and no-one is going to go hungry. They get by through work such as fruit-picking and scrap metal dealing.

This tallied with my observations of the groups who were, at least temporarily, static in the city. Everything was shared; as each person got his or her 'dole' money, it would be pooled with the group, so there was a steady source of income, albeit small, rather than each individual catering for him or herself.

The support was not only material. Along with this went a different perspective on relationships. The tendency within the wider community for some people to dominate others and obtain what was regarded as an unfair share of resources was rejected in favour of mutual decision making.

There was a reaction against relationships in wider society based on power and domination. This was evident in the counter cultures, the work of Dorothy Day and the Catholic Worker Movement, and the local groups, particularly those linked with New Age travellers whom I came to know.

We therefore begin to see the 'marginal' person not as one who has dropped out of society in a negative sense, but as one who is making a constructive critique of society. A deep concern with the relationship between human beings and nature was apparent among those in the counter cultures whom I met, as well as an alternative lifestyle to that of the wider community, as far as interpersonal relationships were concerned.

They see that social inequality and injustice are linked with the control of natural resources; hence the importance attached to a relationship with the natural world. Where it was felt that some had more than their share of such resources, the term used by the street people for helping themselves to such surplus was 'liberation'. For obvious reasons this aspect of their lifestyle could not be followed up.

Since the poor are those excluded from the blessings of God's creation part of the establishing of the Kingdom of God on earth is the opening up of such blessings to the poor. This raises the question of the Christian viewpoint on the relationship between God, man and the created world. While the groups I met were primarily concerned with what they saw to be an unfair distribution of natural resources, there are deeper implications.

According to Kenneth Leech, theologies which separate the natural from the spiritual worlds also tend to be suspicious of the world of politics. The logic of this is clear; lack of concern for the physical world is likely to be accompanied by lack of engagement in it and hence in the daily affairs of the human race. This contrasts with Hebrew theology which was 'deeply committed to the goodness of flesh and matter, seeing human nature as a unity'.[52]

Until the late middle ages there was a spirituality which did link humankind and nature, based on the Genesis account of creation. Examples of this can be seen in the Benedictine tradition of land cultivation, and through Franciscan spirituality.

The statement coming from the margins is a seeking to return to this. While this is implicit in the case of the local groups observed, the work of Dorothy Day and the Catholic Worker Movement in America is a more explicit move in this direction. Their vision was for a return to the land and of the building up of farming communes. Community was the answer, they felt; it had worked for the monastic communities, so why not for lay people with families grouping together.[53]

Here can be seen a potential resolution of the negative view of human nature, put forward by Augustine, without the extremes demonstrated by some cults which have over-reacted against that. Day describes plans for the communes set up by Roman Catholic anarchists[54] which bear a similarity to New Testament Christianity, particularly in the reference to members being subject to one another[55] with community life focusing on the chapel.

Therefore the combined statements of the counter-cultures and those within the Churches whose actions and lifestyle might be regarded as prophetic, have the potential to challenge the Churches. This is another instance of the solution coming from within and bearing some similarity to the theory of "spontaneous order". In *Anarchy in Action* Colin Ward describes this as an important component of the anarchist approach to organisation. Given a common need, a collection of people will, by trial and error, by improvisation and experiment, evolve order out of the situation, 'this order being more durable and more closely related to their needs than any kind of externally imposed authority could provide'.[56]

However, it is recognised that this may not, by itself, lead to the desired utopia. Ward speaks of brief periods when there has been spontaneous order, usually as a result of crises caused by oppressive regimes, such as the 'Prague Spring'.[57] No explanation is given as to why these experiments have not lasted and been reproduced on a larger scale. If the theory were valid, this is what might have been expected.

But the relationship between structures and margins does throw light on this. When structures are not clearly defined, the powers on the margins can be creative; when the structures are defined, they are seen as a threat.[58] Seen in this light the Prague Spring, when the social structures were temporarily in disarray, becomes understandable – as does the reaction when the regime reasserted itself.

From the Church's point of view, with its acceptance of the ultimate authority of God, there is the question as to how this theory of 'spontaneous order' relates to an ultimate spiritual authority.

Ammon Hennacy draws a distinction between spiritual and temporal authority. He says that his idea of God was not an authority whom he obeyed like a monarch but a principle of good as laid down by Jesus in the Sermon on the Mount, which he interpreted in day by day decisions as the forces of the state came in conflict with these ideals. In the same manner every person had to make a choice between his conception of good and of evil.

Temporal and spiritual authority need not be in conflict. There is an incompatibility between anarchism and religion only if the Christian insists on transforming the authoritarian set-up of the Church to the temporal field or the anarchist insists in rejecting authority in religion. In both cases it comes from a confusion of the supernatural with the natural.[59]

It is interesting to speculate how, in practice, one could live with such contrasting views of authority as are to be found in the institutional Roman Catholic Church and the anarchist tradition. Nevertheless, the work of Dorothy Day demonstrates that the relationship between temporal and spiritual authority can be resolved in the Christian tradition.

While recognising the fundamental anarchist view of authority, there is also implicit in Roman Catholic anarchy the recognition that the human race left to its own devices will produce chaos – not order – since that is the nature of the fallen human race. There is therefore the need for a voluntarily accepted spiritual order – as opposed to a temporal order imposed on possibly unwilling subjects – to be found in the recognition of the results of the Fall and recourse to the answer provided by Christ and His Church.

Some street people attempting to adopt facets of an anarchist lifestyle appeared to lack cohesion. The ideals are there, but before too long disputes arise and the group breaks up and re-forms with a changed membership. The question is whether a voluntarily accepted spiritual order would have produced the cohesion that was lacking.

Along with the communal lifestyle of the street people encountered goes a search for a spirituality. This is seen as being an integral part of people's relationship with the land, and the entitlement of each individual to the land and its produce.

The vision of Dorothy Day and her companions of the answer to the problems of urban living, in which oppression leads to poverty, was to return to the land and community living with the sharing that this entailed. There is therefore a convergence between the counter-cultures and those who were taking up a role comparable to early monasticism.

Over and above any practical solution that such communal living offers is the identification with one another. The Incarnation was an entering into the human situation; through touching lepers Jesus himself was contaminated, and so became a marginal person himself. Christian outreach enters into the situation of others and, where those people might be described as 'marginal', there is the identification with that state. Through voluntarily making themselves marginal, they are able to hear those who have not chosen to be so.

IV. The Challenge
from the Margins

A popular criticism of the Churches is that they fail to implement their professed 'option for the poor'. But while there is considerable goodwill that goes unnoticed by such critics, there is the question as to the form this takes. In Chapter II the difficulty experienced with volunteers was outlined; they were ready to do 'good works', but were not prepared to go beyond this to meeting street people on more of an equal footing. It was only a small minority who were prepared to take any steps towards building community with people from such a different background.

At first sight it appeared that the stereotyped views of 'tramps' could be behind this reluctance. But then I found that people who were marginalised in other, very different, ways were experiencing similar treatment.

There was my own experience as a wheelchair user, along with the situation of others with physical disabilities. Many Churches do not have ramped access for wheelchairs, and those who do rarely have reserved parking. In other words, although in theory one might be able to get into the Church, the problem is reaching the Church in the first place. When I pointed out that people who are normally independent, driving their own car, cannot get to Church, the response has been that there are special masses for people with disabilities – but not access to celebrations of the community as a whole.

Then there was the experience of gay Christians. I first heard their account through members of Quest, an organisation for gay Roman Catholics which includes not only active homosexuals but also those who accept, and live according to, the view that only sexual contact between heterosexual married couples is permissible and that therefore they should adopt a celibate lifestyle. Yet again there was a sense of exclusion from the community which, although for different reasons, was similar to the above groups.

This pattern was confirmed when I read 'Outsiders need not apply', an article in *The Tablet*.[60] Thomas Faucher, a Roman Catholic parish priest in the United States, speaks of the obstacles to 'marginalised' people becoming Roman Catholics. On the one hand there are aspects of their life-style; one example was that of a single mother who, because of family and work commitments, was not always free to attend classes which were essential preparation for reception into the Roman Catholic Church; another was a man whose nomadic way of life meant that he was never in one parish long enough to fulfil the requirements. On the other, people in the Church feel uncomfortable with those who are different. He also makes the point that while many parishes help, clothe and feed the poor, they do not want the poor to become the parishioners.

This is but the visible aspect of the problem. In the last chapter, the potential challenge from those on the margins was discussed. The barrier to the formation of relationships was also a hindrance to such statements being heard. There was a mental block inhibiting people from relating to, or hearing from, people on the margins. That this applied to people who were 'different' in such varied ways, suggested that the underlying problem went deeper than discomfort with those whose lifestyle was different.

Since we speak of the 'urban jungle' for the more disrupted areas of cities, it was suggested that the significance of the forest in symbolism and mythology might provide some clues.

The forest/wilderness

The forest represents the unknown and contrasts to settled habitations; it symbolises a marginal state. Linked with the forest is the wilderness. In its primitive sense, 'forest' frequently meant wilderness or an uncultivated tract of country.[61] Some maps refer to Dartmoor and Exmoor as forests, though clearly were never forests in the modern sense of the word. The term 'wilderness' is also interchangeable with 'desert', particularly when it is used in a Middle Eastern context.

This raised the question as to whether there might be a link between the involuntarily marginalised inhabitants of the urban jungle, and the voluntarily marginalised monks of the desert, who had played such an important role in the early days of Christianity.

In popular usage, marginality is seen in negative terms as a state of not belonging. But John Saward, in *Perfect Fools* – a title derived from St Paul's reference to the wisdom of God being at variance with that of the world, in particular being a 'fool' for Christ – emphasises the positive role of marginality.

The anthropological interpretation of the wilderness is described as a point of departure for renewal and reintegration into society. He suggests that the wild life of the madman is a thoroughly natural one in that it enhances his communion with nature and with animals and strengthens his solidarity with others. There is a dichotomy in that while he escapes from human society, his inspired judgements, which emerge from his solitude, are ultimately beneficial to the community. In this respect Saward likens the Irish wild man to the holy men of Syria. The 'strangeness' of the wild man, and his separation from structures endows him with considerable social and spiritual power. There is significance in the relation with the created order; both the Irish *disert* and the Syrian *eremos* could both support life. As such, it was not an enemy. 'The desert may be the place of spiritual battle with the devil, but the monks *love* it.'[62]

The work of Victor Turner is significant in that it demonstrates the essential function of marginality in human experience in general; it is not confined to the realm of Christian spirituality. In *The Ritual Process* he suggests that it is essential that there is a state where people can stand apart temporarily from the social structures, in which they are stripped of status and property, and have an egalitarian relationship irrespective of status in the formal social structures.

Turner uses the term *liminality* to describe the situation of 'threshold people' who are betwixt and between the positions assigned by law, custom, convention and ceremonial, which he also likens to the wilderness. Communitas describes the unstructured or rudimentarily structured society which appears during this liminal phase.[63] The term communitas is used in preference to 'community' to emphasise that it is the relationships, rather than a communal living area, which are of importance.

It is essential for all to enter this as preparation for a changed status in life, at times of crisis, and/or as an annual event. A modern parallel is the custom adopted by many Christians of going into retreat periodically or before a major event.

One purpose of this liminal state is to ensure that relationships are based on shared humanity, rather than on people's roles in the social structure. It thus acts as a safeguard for what occurs in the latter; since all, irrespective of status, have shared this formative experience, there is less likelihood that those in leadership positions will lose contact with the 'grassroots'.

Turner speaks of the sacredness of positions owing their origin to this liminal phase. There are many sacred attributes to certain fixed offices in tribal societies, and some such attributes to every social position. This 'sacred' component is acquired during the *rites de passages*, through which they changed positions. Something of the sacredness of that 'transient humility and modelessness' is carried over into the new status by the incumbent of a higher position or office.

There is therefore a recognition of an essential and generic human bond, without which society could not exist as we know it. 'Liminality implies that the high could not be high unless the low existed, and he who is high must experience what it is like to be low.'[64]

This juxtaposition of the high and the low is not generally evident in the process of selecting and preparing people for leadership in most industrial nations. However, it is of interest to note in the Coronation ceremony for British monarchs, that there is a point at which they are stripped of everything ornate and dressed in a plain white robe prior to their anointing. It appears that this was a reminder of the procedure for crowning kings in ancient Israel. Whether or not this was based on fact, the removal of everything that represented status and wealth was significant.

In Turner's view there is an interdependence between this marginal situation and the social structures which are essential to any society. While on the one hand the immediacy of communitas gives way to the mediacy of structure, on the other, in *rites de passage*, men are released from structure into communitas only to return to structure revitalised by their experience of communitas. 'What is certain is that no society can function adequately without this dialectic'.[65]

Yet marginal situations may also carry a sense of threat. The following comments suggest that while such temporary liminality has a function, when this is sustained, or lacks control from the dominant structure, it then becomes a threat. His view is that for those concerned with the maintenance of "structure", 'all sustained manifestations of communitas must appear as dangerous and anarchical'. Society protects itself from this threat by the imposition of sanctions and conditions. Turner refers to Mary Douglas' view that anything which cannot be clearly classified in terms of traditional criteria or falls between classificatory boundaries, 'is almost everywhere regarded as "polluting" and "dangerous" '.[66]

Relating this to fears of the urban jungle, the people who are there are mostly there for an indefinite period, in a situation beyond the comprehension or control of the wider society.

The 'stranger'

But it is not only the forest *per se* that is feared. The individuals within it are seen as a threat in themselves; 'strangers' are the personification of its unseen powers.[67] In the Birmingham project, it was not only the urban jungle that was feared, but the individuals within it were each viewed as a threat. It is possible to see this 'threat' become apparent when a new-comer moves into a neighbourhood of well established residents. The newcomer may be regarded with suspicion until he/she can demonstrate that he/she subscribes to the values of the dominant group.

I had a student on placement, and as part of his learning experience he visited Churches and Church-based agencies as though he were homeless. When attending day centres, he was conscious of the gap between 'us' and 'them', in that the volunteer helpers were, for the most part, more comfortable giving practical help, such as serving refreshments, than conversing in the way that would be expected in most social gatherings. In addition to visiting such centres, he also went on his own to places such as vicarages where it is customary for homeless people to call for cups of tea. From the way he was received it was apparent that, even when well away from the environment of the urban jungle, he as an individual was seen as a threat.

It is when the 'stranger' meets people from the dominant society that the nature of the threat he, or she, represents is seen. In myths, legends, folk-tales and in literature generally, the 'stranger' is frequently the one destined to replace the reigning power in a country or locality. 'He stands for the possibility of unseen change, for the future made present, or for mutation in general.'[68]

This possibility of unseen change finds a dramatic expression when Jacob wrestles with the stranger[69] and finds he has been wrestling with God, with the implication this had for his future. The stranger tells him that from then on his name will be Israel, indicating that he will become the father of God's chosen people.

Strangers are the personification of the unknown. They do not fit into a precise category; they are neither in nor out. They are defined as being 'unpredictable, bearers of power but also of possible pollution to the society as a whole. People in such a position may be thought, often rightly, to be upsetting, endangering the society; they need to be guarded against;

but they may also be a source of blessing, of new strength and wisdom'.[70]

In traditional societies, the danger would be controlled by rituals governing the person's re-entry into society. Therefore, according to Mary Douglas, it is up to others to take precautions against the danger from such a person.[71] The difficulties encountered by social workers when trying to integrate people who have been in prison, mental hospital, or have demonstrated in other ways that they are outside the accepted boundaries of society, illustrate this.

In Western society there are no rituals by which such people may be reintegrated, which may explain why many remain in a state of marginality. Yet, while there may be no formal rituals for integration, there are processes by which certain groups of marginal people may gain a measure of acceptance, once their lifestyle has been subjected to some form of negotiated control.

The contrast between the treatment of gypsy travellers and New Age travellers demonstrates the difference between those who have gained such acceptance and those who have not. While some tolerance has built up towards gypsy travellers, with certain conditions for coexistence having developed over the years, this is not the case with New Age travellers. *Roaming Free* was a documentary programme about different kinds of travellers in BBC 1's *Heart of the Matter* series. Whereas the situation of gypsy travellers illustrated the comments quoted by Turner and Douglas above, concerning classification in terms of traditional criteria and being subjected to conditions by the wider society, the New Age travellers did not, in spite of similarities in terms of outward lifestyle.

Two significant comments were made towards the end of the programme concerning the underlying reasons for opposition to the New Age travellers. The Rev David Penney, Social Responsibility Officer for the Salisbury Diocese, referred to people's fears that New Age travellers might be carriers of HIV or AIDS, child molesters, or drug barons. But he went on to say he thought that behind all that was the feeling that people had to protect their children from the temptation of joining the travellers because they felt it was difficult at times to defend their own culture.

Chris, a New Age traveller, picks this point up, saying that the reason for wanting to stop the festivals which brought the travellers together are not those given. Rather, people who are leading dreary existences might visit the travellers and be attracted by their lifestyle, thus questioning the social fabric of society as a whole.

Whether marginal people are sources of pollution or power depends, not only on their situation, but also on that of the wider society. The social system is alive with creative, sustaining powers when the formal structure is weak, but when the structures are clearly defined, pollution can become a danger, according to Mary Douglas.[72]

Where there are strong structures acceptance of marginal people is less likely to occur. In my experience there appeared to be two factors at play among those Church groups which experienced the greatest difficulty in relating to street people. Firstly, the more 'clerical' the particular Church from which they came, the less confidence volunteers had in their ability to undertake the work. Secondly, and more significantly, the more the parent Church was identified with specific national or cultural communities the less inclined its members were to relate to people who were not part of that community. As such, they tended to be tightly knit groups, concerned with maintaining their culture and links with their countries of origin; the Church became, for them, not only a spiritual, but a social base in which it was difficult for others to have a full part.

Social psychologists have studied the relationship problems between 'in-groups' and 'out-groups'[73] and the discussion in the Church Growth Movement, concerning the 'homogeneous unit principle' also points to the way in which cultural bonds in a Church may inhibit relationships with those outside that particular group.

Marginality in a biblical perspective

This link between the prevailing social structure and the perception of marginality, can be seen in the Judaeo-Christian
tradition.

The alternative community of Moses, with its relationships
of mutuality, sets the scene for the Christian era, according
to Walter Brueggemann's *The Prophetic Imagination.*

The ministry of Moses represented a radical departure
from the regime of the Egyptian pharaohs and brought
about a new social reality. That social reality, as will be
seen, was one that not only identified with marginal people, but saw such solidarity as a great virtue. According
to Brueggemann Israel can only be understood in terms
of this new call of God and the assertion of an 'alternative social reality'.[74]

The alternative consciousness which came about through
the leadership of Moses was characterised by 'criticising
and energising'.[75] But this went beyond any cosmetic
exercise; it was concerned with change at the deepest level.
Moses was not struggling to transform a regime; his concern was with the consciousness that undergirded and made
such a regime possible. He was also 'concerned not with
societal betterment through the repentance of the regime but
rather with totally dismantling it in order to permit a new
reality to appear'.[76]

Brueggemann links the alternative community with the
wilderness, these being where Moses' alternative community
was formed.[77] This points to the significance of the wilderness elsewhere in the Bible; it was in the wilderness that
John the Baptist prepared the way for the coming of Jesus,
and it was the wilderness to which Jesus himself went to
prepare for his ministry. This resembles Turner's temporary liminality from which people emerge prepared for a new
situation.

The wilderness, and the marginality that it symbolises,
is the place from which power emanates. Jesus and
John the Baptist could be viewed as the 'stranger' who
has been in contact with that power with the degree of

power or threat depending on the existing social structures. To the ruling authority, this represented a threat, as can be seen from the opposition that arose. To those who were not an integral part of the ruling structure, it was a potential source of power.

In contrast to this alternative community, the reign of Solomon was characterised by well-being and affluence, which was in part made possible by oppressive social policy.[78] In speaking of the 'happiness' of Solomon's reign, Brueggemann draws attention to the contrast between the happiness of affluence and that of freedom. Where there is immunity to any transcendent voice and disregard of neighbour, passion will finally disappear. 'And where passion disappears there will not be any serious humanizing energy'.[79]

Solomon's regime aimed at the self-securing of king and dynasty.[80] Among the measures to achieve this were the centralisation of the tax system through tax districts displacing the role of clans and tribes, an elaborate bureaucracy, and a standing army.

Such a centralised, hierarchical structure leaves little room for the maintenance of equilibrium ensured by the liminal stage. While Brueggemann does not go as far as Mary Douglas in explicitly referring to any threat from the margins when structures are strong, it is evident that the effect of this centralised structure and emphasis on affluence rather than freedom, was to limit the opportunity for 'energising'. Solomon's social vision was a far cry from that of Moses; any possibility of an alternative consciousness or an alternative community was minimised.

Brueggemann describes the contrast between the relationships in Moses' alternative community and those during Solomon's reign. This reflects the contrast between the relationships which take place in communitas, based on shared humanity, and those in structures in which people relate on the basis of their roles in that structure. Solomon had exchanged a 'vision of freedom' for the 'reality of security'. A community of neighbours was reduced to a society in which all were subservient; covenanting was replaced with consuming, and 'all promises had been reduced to tradable commodities'.

The comment that 'Every such trade-off made real energy less likely'[81] is particularly significant in that it points to the changing relationship between the margins and society's structures. As the latter become more rigid there is less room for dialectic between the two.

Brueggemann draws a contrast between the freedom and accessibility of God, apparent in Moses' alternative community, with the role of the temple under Solomon. As the temple became part of the royal landscape, access to God was controlled by the king and those to whom he granted access. This arrangement clearly served two interrelated functions. It gave the king the liberty to do whatever he wished, since there was no means of resisting, and in giving the king such a monopoly, it ensured that no marginal person could approach God except on the king's terms. 'There will be no disturbing cry against the king here.'[82]

This control of access to God, as the structure becomes increasingly hierarchical, is echoed in the history of the Christian Church. Guiseppe Alberigo describes how, in his view, the mediation of the priesthood takes the place of the *ecclesia* as a whole as structures evolve. 'Salvation came to be sought less and less through the *ecclesia*, as the community of the baptised, and more and more through an individual religious relationship mediated through the priesthood.'[83]

The 'criticising and energising' of the prophets, took place against the background of the regime of Solomon, and other repressive regimes. The birth of Jesus brought an end to this and inaugurated a new situation for marginal people that was beyond what had been imaginable in their previous situation.

This contrast, between rigid structures on the one hand, and the alternative community linked with receptivity to prophecy on the other, can also be seen in different perceptions of humility. Klaus Wengst, in *Humility: the Solidarity of the Humiliated*, shows that humility can be seen either 'from above', i.e. from the perspective of those in power, or 'from below', i.e. from a viewpoint of solidarity with the 'humiliated', according to the prevailing ethos in society. Along with these two understandings of humility go contrasting attitudes towards marginal people.

In viewing humility 'from above' the Graeco-Roman tradition equates humility to lowly social position, lowly disposition of insignificant people. Upward social mobility, seen as a virtue in this tradition, is a way out of humility.

But humility, seen 'from below' in the Old Testament-Jewish tradition, presents a picture of the 'alternative community' suggestive of that described by Brueggemann. In contrast to the Greek and Roman interpretation, the Old Testament texts speak from the perspective of these insignificant people and take the side of the 'underdog'. Wengst gives a number of general examples of God's solidarity with the oppressed.[84] He also points more specifically to the connection between riches, power and injustice on the one hand and lowly social status and laudable ethical conduct on the other,[85] and to God standing on the side of the poor against the rich. Wengst quotes Psalm 37 and suggests that although the writer is not one of the disadvantaged, he speaks on their behalf. Related to this is the view that the virtue of humility is the modesty of the rich, and the way they treat the poor.[86]

In the understanding of the tradition of humility in the Qumran we begin to see the mutuality of relationships which point the way to the early Christian community. Wengst demonstrates that in the Qumran texts is to be found a mutuality, if not equality, with a monastic-type community as the framework in which each exhorts/encourages one another in truthfulness, humility and steadfast love.

In Wengst, as in Brueggemann, this mutuality of relationships in the alternative community bears a resemblance to Turner's communitas which carries over into the early days of Christianity. Mary's Magnificat shows God's solidarity with the humiliated and, while the Epistle of James includes the rich in the community, they are not only not to expect privileges, but are also to be generous to those less well off.

Humility is therefore the basis on which members of the community relate to one another, reflecting the mutuality of relationships which were evident in the Qumran community.

St Paul does not invite the better-off to imitate his lifestyle; that is part of his apostolic existence. But he does exhort all to solidarity with the insignificant. Wengst quotes Romans 12.16: 'Do not be haughty, but associate with the lowly'. This is followed by a reference to the exhortation to people not to be wise on their own account. This would be wisdom gained apart from others and looking for upward mobility, which would disrupt solidarity and lead to competition. Paul speaks of the need for harmony within the community, but this can only come about if 'the community is orientated on the possibilities, the needs and the distress of its weakest members – if it allows itself to 'descend' with them, is in solidarity with them'.[87]

The 'alternative community' becomes particularly apparent in Wengst's comments on Philippians 2.1-11. Against this background of Roman society's concern with upward social mobility Paul invites the community as a whole, not just isolated individuals, to behave in the opposite way to that prevalent in society. Those who were 'in Christ' thus become another society, an alternative society which shows solidarity. This demonstrates 'humility' not as individual renunciation but as a building block for a new society which can be all-embracing since its values are based on solidarity, not hierarchical relationships.

The use of the term 'alternative' here suggests a radical departure from prevailing attitudes. It is interesting to compare this with Brueggemann's view that Moses was not merely reforming, but dismantling, the existing order.

Wengst gives further examples of relationships based on mutuality from the epistles to the Colossians and Ephesians. He comments that 'Humility is thus the opposite of any form of making oneself an absolute . . .',[88] and so, it may be added, humility is in direct contrast to the 'royal consciousness' of Solomon.

The conclusion is a clear statement of the Christian's relationship with the 'humiliated', who would include marginal people. Wengst emphasises the need to recall the practice of 'humility' shown by Jesus and the majority of primitive Christianity, and its origins which go far back into the Old Testament-Jewish tradition, according to which humility 'is not a virtue of subjects, but denotes the solidarity of the humiliated'.[89]

To summarise, two factors emerge which influence the perception of this marginal state.

Firstly, there is the degree of permanence of the state of marginality; secondly, there is the degree to which the prevailing structures are either weak or strong, i.e. hierarchical. Were this to be plotted graphically, with these two conditions as axes, two significant clusters would appear. The most threatening would be those who were permanently marginalised in a society with strong structures; the most creative would be temporary marginality when structures were loose. Street people could be situated in the former cluster. Turner's liminal phase, with the relationships which take place in communitas would be found in the most creative cluster.

Turner's contention is that the liminal phase is essential to maintain equilibrium in the wider structures. The question this poses is that, where the state of liminality/communitas is not built-in to a society, it may emerge as a reaction against the resulting lack of equilibrium, as did the alternative community of Moses in reaction to the Egyptian regime. A further question is whether the Christian Church has this function in relation to the human race as a whole. The above discussion points in this direction through demonstrating that the true virtue of humility is that of solidarity with the 'underdog', as opposed to being linked with subservience in hierarchical relationships.

That power lies in such marginality emerged from the work of Mary Douglas; the above discussion has suggested that the ministry of Jesus was an expression of power coming from the margins.

Yet it is apparent from the experiences recounted in Chapter

II that the Church has distanced itself from the state of creative marginality. According to Wengst, signs of a shift are detectable in the first century. That which makes the term 'humility' so suspect today – its prime associations with subservience and servile obedience – emerges at this stage.

In his first letter to the Community in Corinth, Clement points to this. There had been a rebellion against the leadership of the Church in Corinth, and the letter interprets 'humility' as unconditional submission to authority, along the lines of the Graeco-Roman tradition.

This suggests a reversal of humility as the basis for a community of solidarity, and a return to an understanding of humility which underpins the development and establishment of hierarchical structures. Wengst concludes that while the understanding of humility as obedient subservience had only emerged latterly in primitive Christianity, '. . . it is this understanding of "humility" which has had the most powerful effect in Church history. . . .'[90]

A link can be seen between the way this understanding of humility may be used to exercise control, and the correlation between a redemption-centred theology and authoritarian regimes discussed in Chapter III. Wengst goes on to refer to Heinrich Heine's view of Roman Catholicism with its emphasis on subservience as 'the best-tried support of despotism. . . .'[91]

However, it is not only in the Roman Catholic Church that views which support the status quo are to be found. The Protestant ethic, relating poverty to spiritual turpitude, has been seen to undermine the possibility of solidarity with those who have not made it in a competitive society.[92]

Each is approaching the question from a different perspective, which cannot be fully analysed here; the significant point is that doctrinal stances are being used to identify and control potential threats to the status quo. Related to this is the way access to God may be controlled, as suggested by the views of Brueggemann and Alberigo.

Control by the structures is therefore exercised in more

than one way; the one focuses on the competence of the individual, the other concerns his/her access to God.

This brings us back to the paradox – between what appears to be the dominant biblical model on the one hand, and reactions from within the Churches to threats from the margins, on the other. Part of this paradox is that marginal situations, such as the desert, have traditionally been the place of renewal for the Church. The question therefore is one of entering the margins, not only to meet those already there, but because it is the place of power.

V. Entering the Urban Desert

Life in the desert is physically tough and demanding. We also know that it can be demanding in other ways. Yet, from Kenneth Leech's experience of some agencies who seek to work among those on the margins of society, there are those who, through fear, avoid the rigours of the journey. Using this analogy, they would like to travel in an air-conditioned coach, taking with them their familiar creature comforts. They would not venture far from the coach, let alone share the life of those whom they have gone to visit.

This is illustrated by the experience of girls I took into my house when they were trying to relate to people in the Church I was attending. The parishioners were ready to preach to them, or give practical help, but not to get alongside them in order to hear the underlying hurt. This is similar to the effect of the two models of 'caring' which Leech uses to illustrate the way people in the Churches keep their distance, outlined in Chapter I.

Each in its own way creates barriers. In the 'liberal professional' model there is a distinction – and distance – between the professional and the client; in the 'crusading' model the person sent to preach is distinct from those to whom he or she preaches. Both these models fall short of a truly incarnational approach which by entering into the situation of others and sharing their pain – as Jesus did through his Incarnation and Passion – touches people at their point of need.

I would suggest that in some instances pastoral work, and much of Church-based social work, has taken on board the methodology and values of secular social work. We need greater clarity when distinguishing between the role of the social worker and care by the community, particularly the Christian one. In the case of the former, there is a problem to be solved, and the 'professional' has a body of skill and knowledge which the 'client' needs to draw on in order to resolve this. While there is a clear need for this kind of intervention, the role of the social worker must not be confused with that of the caring community, in particular with the fostering of relationships which affirm the whole person.

Other professions have clearer boundaries as to where their role begins and ends. For example, most people understand the role of the lawyer, doctor, and accountant. But it seems that with the breakdown of communities, the expectation of society is that social workers will do what would formerly have been undertaken by neighbours.

At one stage in my work as a social worker, I was concerned with the elderly. My 'patch' covered two very different areas. One was an old, long-established, inner-city community; when difficulties occurred the neighbours would immediately rally around. By contrast, the other area included a new housing estate where the elderly could be in difficulty without anyone knowing.

Along with this, many people have lost the ability to listen to others; listening in itself is affirming because it makes the person being listened to feel that they, and what they have to say, are worthwhile.

It is this kind of neighbourliness and listening which are the foundation for basic human love. A professional social worker, with dozens of cases, each with a range of problems, cannot be a substitute for that. At one point I and my social work assistant had a joint case-load of around three hundred elderly people We could not be good neighbours ourselves but, through liaising with voluntary groups in the local community, we could see that there were good neighbours available and be a safety net when situations arose with which such neighbours could not cope.

In the aftermath of the Dunblane massacre the clergy, rather than taking over, were enabling the community as a whole to respond. While this situation differs in many respects from that of the 'marginal' people we are considering, the significant point is that it was relationships within the community which were seen to facilitate 'healing'. It was not the task of professionals on their own.

This brings us to the central theme of this discussion – the Christian's solidarity with the marginalised. This is a focal point for Thomas Merton, particularly in his later days as will be discussed below; the marginal position of the monk gave him a particular identification with other marginal people. What Merton says of the monk could also be applied to any practising Christian if one accepts that Christians are 'strangers'. Kenneth Leech sums this up:

> Ministry to those whom society has rejected and marginalised must begin with a recognition and an exploration of our own marginal status as Christ's disciples.[93]

A person's own vulnerability is reinforced by encounters with those on the streets. The situation of the latter appeared to be an unwelcome reminder of the vulnerability of that familiar lifestyle, in that many are aware of those within their own circle who, if not literally on the streets, have been reduced to difficult circumstances, for example as a result of alcoholism, or redundancy. The street people were a living expression of fears people may have for themselves. This echoes Jung's theory, referred to in the previous chapter, concerning the forest representing our unconscious fears.

Looked at from another angle, it is a reminder of John Saward's comments about the significance of the presence of the poor as visitors to Cistercian monasteries. He describes how the original aim of the founders of Citeaux was to enable the monk to become like one of the *anawim* of the Old Testament, one of God's poor, voluntarily stripped of everything. They were called to experience poverty in a way such that their physical poverty was a sign of that total dispossession which Jesus describes as the only way to eternal life. While possessions cause people to cling to economic power and privilege, this is the reverse of Jesus' way of self-abandonment.

Saward describes the material dispossession of the poor man as 'the efficacious sign of that total dispossession which is faith: 'dying with Christ, sharing his sufferings in order to know the power of his resurrection'.[94] Translated into the situation of work among people whose worldly possessions are carried everywhere in shopping bags, and who are regularly treated with contempt by people in general and officialdom in particular, it is a challenge to our dependency upon status and possessions. It is not so much that these are harmful in themselves, but it is when they, rather than our relationship with God, become the source of our self-esteem that the dependency needs to be challenged.

Kenneth Leech's description in *Care and Conflict*, of St John of the Cross's Dark Night of the Soul bears some relation to the concept of temporary liminality and the wilderness.[95]

He describes the Dark Night as a sharing of Christ's self-emptying, a 'process of disillusionment . . . the undermining of the false self . . . a process of liberation through disillusionment' and the disintegration of defences which mask the true self.[96] While St John of the Cross did not himself relate the Dark Night of the Soul to marginality, the freeing from illusions is a characteristic of the desert, according to the definition given in the previous chapter.[97]

It has been suggested that the encounter with those on the margins entails an entering into a wilderness or desert experience before engagement can occur. The symbolic significance of the desert has been shown to have common ground with the 'urban jungle', indicating that the latter itself offers a desert experience.

There are three facets of the wilderness/desert which point towards this comparison with the urban jungle.

Firstly, the lifestyle, if not the geographic locality, of inhabitants of the urban jungle contrasts with that of those in established settlements. In Chapter I street people have been described. The flaws in society, of which their situation is the result, bear some resemblance to the involuntarily marginalised to be found in the desert. In her Introduction to *The Lives of the Desert Fathers* Benedicta Ward describes people who were in the desert to avoid the slavery that had resulted from an unjust taxation system and those who were conscientious objectors to military service.[98] While they might not be the victims of the same injustices, if it is accepted that street people's situation is not entirely of their own making but is the result of family breakdown combined with wider factors, then it, like that of those in the desert, can be attributed to social dislocation.

As far as voluntary marginality is concerned, Turner and Douglas' comments about the role of temporary liminality, mentioned in the previous chapter, are paralleled by the prophetic role of the Church; each is interacting with the wider society, keeping it mindful of what is happening on the margins. That this voluntary marginal state is not widely evident in the urban jungle points to Leech's analysis of the need to enter this state if there is to be dialogue with the involuntarily marginalised.

Secondly, it is on the one hand a place of spiritual battle (with the devil) and on the other a place of encounter with God.

In meeting street people one is confronted with the effects of disruptive forces at work in the wider society. Bishop David Jenkins in *The Contradiction of Christianity* suggests that the way the poor are treated as less than human reveals the essentially dehumanising trends at work throughout society. Marginal people, not only the physically underprivileged, are not just one of society's problems. Their situation and deprivations are *the* problem of society. As such 'they are signs of the judgment of the Kingdom'.[99]

Additionally, many street drug addicts could be described as victims of a particular kind of exploitation. As has been seen in the definition of street people, there are those who take to drugs to deaden emotional pain. Such people are targeted by the drug pushers; they may become addicted, and then take up a criminal lifestyle in order to support their habit. The extent to which such vulnerable people are targeted is not something which has been thoroughly documented, but is generally accepted by those working at street level.

There is therefore a sense in which, in encountering the situation of street people, one is encountering the effects of defects in society. There are the structural defects contributing to their situation, and these are compounded by those who are prone to abusing drugs being a target for drug dealers and others who can exploit their vulnerable situation.

Conversely, it has been shown that the place of marginality is a place of encounter with God. Therefore it follows that as the urban jungle is a place of marginality, it, too, is potentially a meeting place with God.

Thirdly, it is a place of freedom from illusions; it is also a place of freedom from captivity, i.e. the place to which the people of Israel went from Egypt. To liken the urban jungle to a place of freedom from captivity might seem strange in that there are senses in which it is a place of captivity to many, but the 'freedom' in question is that from false realities.

Among the noticeable characteristics of street people are their lack of material possessions, evidenced by their worldly goods in two or three plastic bags. There is also their lack of status, as demonstrated by the way they are treated by those in authority. John Saward's description of the poor visiting the Cistercian monasteries serving as a sign of the stripping of self before God is mentioned above.[100]

Entering into the world of the marginalised entails this stripping or removal of false reality which has been seen to be part of the desert experience.

This parallel between the desert and the urban jungle is illustrated by a letter I received from a Carmelite nun describing how her former existence as a 'street junkie' had been a desert experience.

What had begun as seeming freedom in anonymity ended in alienation. . . . I had created a barren and painful desert for myself, and I had help creating it from the society in which I lived. It was and is a culture or lack of culture built on utilitarian principles not on persons, on technological progress without the necessary wisdom to make the best human decisions. And God used the alienation and betrayals to bring me to my senses, to lead me into a fruitful desert. . . .

Similar stories of other former street people demonstrate the effect of the starkness of the urban jungle, in which they found themselves confronted with the results of a breakdown in social structures in the wider society, and thrown back on their own internal resources.[101] Each goes through a form of darkness, the removal of illusions and emerges with a new sense of reality.

But there are also those who have chosen the inner city, such as some monastic communities who have set up houses in deprived areas. The effect of this has demonstrated the role of the urban jungle in the 'formation' of those who have entered it.

One such example is a house, set up by Worth Abbey of the English Benedictine Congregation, in Lima, Peru, where the monks lived and ran a parish in a poor part of the city. This contrasted with the mainstream of the English Benedictine Congregation which is primarily known for running boys' public schools.

Two monks have commented on the effect of being part of the Peruvian community. Fr. Fabian Glencross writes of his experience in Peru:

What is happening is that I am gradually stepping back into the real world again, with all its struggle between people, and I realize that what I have avoided for so long, the purpose for which I built the craft in the first place, has a name and is something many of us stylish intellectual people hate so much. It is POVERTY.[102]

What he means by 'poverty' in this context, of a book on monasticism, has to do not so much with material poverty *per se* as with poverty as one of the religious vows, with all that that entails of the stripping of self of dependence on material possessions and status, as an aid to poverty of spirit.

He goes on to describe how he took off his sixteenth-century monastic habit; the remarks that follow suggest that, to him, this was part of a barrier between himself and the rest of the world. He found that the people whom he was supposed to be there to help knew more about humility in the face of adversity and courage and self-discipline in the midst of personal difficulty than he had learned in thirty years of hiding behind a mask. He found that the theology he knew was being overturned and that the basic Christian truths had to be looked at with a new honesty.

From this one sees that it was the urban desert, not traditional monasticism, which was for him the decisive desert experience. To him, the latter had been a flight from reality, rather than a flight to reality.

Another Benedictine monk from Worth Abbey also found life in the Lima house proved to be a turning point in his priestly life. John Bolton was acting as parish priest and as such playing the role of the person in control. He describes how he was sitting there 'quite smugly' when the co-ordinator from his sector of the parish stood up, pointed out that while all the planning was good, he wanted to ask when John Bolton was going to 'stop working for us and start working with us?' From this it became quite clear that one had to sit and listen to what people were saying.[103]

This demonstrates a return to a relationship of mutuality, and away from that of the priestly caste distinct from the laity. The encounter with the urban jungle had brought about a stripping of dependence upon a position of power which bears some resemblance to what happened to Fabian Glencross.

Austin Smith, a Passionist Father, set up the Passionist Inner City Mission in Liverpool 8, intended to be a 'presence' in the inner city. He found that those in the inner city were speaking to him. He was conscious that he must do something for the inner city, but he gradually became aware 'that the inner city was about to demand a revolution in me'.[104]

He begins his 'First reflections' on this by describing some of the creativity he found in the Inner City. He found hope in the centre of hopelessness, and so many local people striving to recreate life. While in the middle of a wounded world, he could hear:

the heartbeat of God's creation. I was challenged to make sure that I received from this world before I could in any sense act or indeed live with relevancy'.[105]

In encountering the situation of the marginalised in the inner city he states that it is hard to tolerate an apologia which underpins such a state of society. Compassion is not enough by itself; there is 'a crying need for collaboration'. While he did not feel he could become identified with the poor of this world, he could at least be identified with 'the struggle of the poor for their liberation'.[106]

Following his comment about becoming identified with the struggle of the poor for their liberation, he says that if he is to accept that challenge, then he had to face a radical change in his own life.

Again, a stepping away from the clergy-laity divide can be seen with a return to mutuality, and the challenge this presents to the individual concerned. Additionally, there are indications of the 'counter-culture'; of not only suffering with, but struggling with, marginal people.

Some monastic communities have been more explicit in their recognition of the comparison between the desert and the 'urban jungle'. For example, Brother James Kennedy, of the ecumenical monastic Community of the Transfiguration in the Spanish quarter of Albuquerque, New Mexico, describes the ministry of his community in which the concept of the urban jungle as a modern equivalent of the desert has become a reality. He sees the contemporary city as the desert; a place to which people are called in order to empty themselves of selfish pursuits and to experience the self-emptying and poverty of the crucified Lord. He describes the noisy streets of the inner-city as their cloister, the 'wilderness of human hearts' as their desert. Their hermit's cell is the deep centre of the heart where they seek to foster an interior life of union with the Holy Trinity.[107]

A significant development is currently taking place within the Carmelite tradition. A group of Carmelite monks and nuns have established hermitages in the Colorado desert, thus reverting to the earliest traditions of monasticism. There is a link with the involuntarily marginalised and the urban jungle through a community of Franciscans in the Bronx with whom they interchange.

This new development is an attempt to revive the counter-culture element in monasticism. The founder, William McNamarra, sees an intimate relationship between real, live monasticism and the socio-political world. He describes how originally the vows of obedience and poverty represented ways of transcending and criticizing a conventional loyalty to *status quo* power arrangements and the reification of people in servitude to an unjust economic system. Previously the monastic vows exemplified a quality of relationship and communal equity beyond the experience of either the oppressed victims or their masters. If indeed politics is 'the science of the possible', then monasticism should be a real alternative, and thus make an enormous contribution to the future direction of political and economic organisation.[108]

A link can be seen between monasticism, the counter-cultures, and the urban jungle. It has been suggested in Chapter III that the prophetic role has been taken up by the counter-cultures. This link between the counter-cultures and the prophetic role of monasticism is discussed by Thomas Merton in an appendix 'Notes on the Future of Monasticism' in *Contemplation in a World of Action*. He speaks of monks and nuns as:

> people who have consciously and deliberately adopted a mode of life which is marginal with respect to the rest of society, implicitly critical of that society, seeking a certain distance from that society and a freedom from its domination and its imperatives, but nevertheless open to its needs and in dialogue with it.[109]

Merton finds an affinity with the intellectual who does not have a vested interest in the establishment and is critical of it. He sees that such people have taken over from the mediaeval role of the monk, friar and clerk. They are free to move around and have ideas of their own. Additionally, such people are aware of and open to the underclass. He sees these as being close to monastics, and very interested in them, visiting monasteries to see if they have something they can respect.[110]

He illustrates this prophetic role by describing an encounter with European revolutionary students in California to whom he introduced himself as a monk. A French revolutionary student leader replied 'We are monks also'. He sees in this statement a neglected aspect of the monastic vocation, bearing in mind his definition of monasticism. While the criticism is different, the common ground was that both had seen that the claims of the world are fraudulent.[111]

There is therefore the potential for a coming together of the successors of the desert hermits with both the involuntarily marginalised, and those who occupy a position equivalent to that of Turner's 'temporary liminality', in the urban jungle.

The experiences of firstly individuals then religious communities encountering the desert experience have been outlined. The implication is that while the individual may be called upon to pass through this 'Dark Night', the same may be true for institutions. Kenneth Leech refers to the views of Gilbert Shaw, formerly warden of the Community of the Sisters of the Love of God in Oxford, who believed that there was not only a 'Dark Night' of the (individual) soul, but also a Dark Night of institutions. Like Shaw, Leech believes that the contemporary situation is a challenge, not simply to individuals, but to institutions among which the Church must be included. As long as Christian faith and life are identified with the values of dominant cultures, 'the collapse of one will be synonymous with the other'.[112]

The ending of persecution 'weakened the eschatological expectation and the feeling of being "strangers" in society'.[113] That could well describe much of contemporary Church life with its identification with the values of the broader society.

It is a logical step, then, to see that it is not only individuals, but a group, whether it is a local Church, or the Church as a whole, which must face the challenge of the desert. This becomes apparent in the experience of the East Harlem Protestant Parish, New York, as described in Bruce Kenrick's *Come out the Wilderness,* so named from a Negro spiritual,

> We feel like ashoutin' as we
> Come out the wilderness
> Leanin' on the Lord

He describes how a group of Christians, from different Church backgrounds, settled in East Harlem to establish a Church there; the title is a self-explanatory link with the wilderness. They found themselves actively involved in the lives and difficulties of those around them, and in political action to rectify some of the conditions which prevailed.

A significant point was the effect that this had on them as a parish, and how it challenged them, as set out in an address by one of the pastors on the parable of the grain of wheat which falls into the ground, is buried, and then bears fruit; his words could well be addressed to any congregation, or to the Church as a whole:

> . . . That's the choice. We can live on the surface: we can close our doors on the fouled-up lives of those around us, and keep clean as we wither away and die. Or we can follow Christ, and bury ourselves deep in the dirt of a world that is needy and sinful and terribly real: and then at last we can take root and live and mature and bear fruit. . . .[114]

The view of Aloysius Pieris S.J. that the teaching magisterium and pastoral magisterium 'are impotent unless cross-fertilised by the magisterium of the poor' encapsulates much of what has been said above. This authority of the poor arises from the fact that they have no-one else to rely on except God. God therefore becomes a real experience to whom they turn for everything; by contrast the rest of us have other gods on whom we rely, who give us comfort and security, 'and even our fight for survival is based upon these other gods upon whom we depend'.

I would suggest that among those other gods are status, power and possessions. That is what entering the wilderness, the desert, or the liminal phase, counteracts. Pieris also says that 'When you are in touch with the poor you become very normal, you really develop'.[115]

This confirms the view that building community in

solidarity with those on the margins of society goes further than the provision of material help. It is the way by which the Church is true to its roots in the incarnate life of Jesus, through which He entered, and struggled with, the human situation in order to give it new life and hope.

To summarise, we can point to two aspects to the process of entering the urban desert.

Firstly, there is the stripping of false reality, which comes of being socialised into a structure where relationships are based on roles as opposed to the shared humanity experienced in 'communitas'. This amounts to meeting the 'other' in their 'otherness', an approach which Emmanuel Lévinas describes as one contrasting with that which takes over the 'other'.[116] Yet, as Leech points out, as does Jean Vanier,[117] this involves becoming vulnerable and experiencing the pain of growth. This process can be seen in the accounts of some of the individuals described above; Fabian Glencross and Austin Smith in particular speak of the effect of the 'urban jungle' on them.

Secondly, once that solidarity has been established, there is the capacity to hear the statements coming from the margins. The counter-cultures have a potential role in this, according to both Leech and Merton.

Thomas Merton in particular suggests that this entails a new alignment of monks with the counter-cultures since the latter have taken on the role of criticising the world and its structures. While this could be queried on the grounds that certain counter-cultures, such as the Children of God,[118] have adopted a lifestyle which could not be regarded as expressions of 'gospel values', yet even in such instances the question has to be asked as to why they came into existence in the first place.

It could be argued that what Merton says of the monastic vocation applies to Christians as a whole, since, from the biblical model, solidarity with those on the margins was the role of all, not of any particular group.

While traditional spirituality has spoken to the individual's growth, it became apparent from the discussion at the end of Chapter IV that it is not individuals in isolation who are hesitant to enter the desert, but that the Church as a whole has formed an in-built resistance to what emanates from the margins. Hence the relevance of Gilbert Shaw's concept of the 'Dark Night of institutions'. That that is feasible on more than an individual basis was indicated by the Harlem Church.

There is therefore a mission in reverse, emanating from the 'magisterium of the poor'. The Church does not only enter the world of marginal people in order to change their situation; it enters that area in order to be first changed itself.

VI. And on to the Promised Land?

More significant than the existence of distance between people in the Churches and those on the streets are the factors that have created that distance. The role that structure plays in this is a recurring theme throughout the discussion. Therefore, in looking at the conclusions that might be drawn, and signposts for the way forward, the question of structure is a starting point.

Initially, there were the implications of the problem-centred approach of most social care agencies. An interpretation that could be put upon this is that such agencies, linked to the prevailing social structures, are seeking to reintegrate those who belong to it, but have a problem which is interfering with their capacity to function within it. Once the problem is solved, they will function within such structures. Such provisions appeared to fall short of meeting the needs of those whose 'problem' was that they fell outside the structures of that society.

The discussion on the relationship between the Churches and street people demonstrated that street people constituted a distinct social group, not only outside the prevailing social structures but also outside those of the Churches of the second stage of the Church, as defined by Vincent Donovan. It was suggested that there were therefore grounds for regarding street people as belonging to the third stage of the Church.

But a distinct aspect of the situation of street people, as well as their general position in that third stage, was the threat they were seen to pose to those within the main structures of society. Moreover, not only were street people themselves seen as a threat, but, from the experience of William Booth, there were indications that those who had attempted to work in marginal situations were also regarded as a threat. This suggested that the marginal state itself, not only those within it, represented a threat which affected people who had contact with it, regardless of their origin.

A significant factor, therefore, was the element of conflict between that marginal state and the prevailing structures. The use of the term 'counter-culture' is in itself suggestive of conflict. This highlights a contrast between street people and other groups belonging to the third stage. Whereas most Third World communities are communities in their own right, and a source of self-esteem, a counter culture is, as the term suggests, a form of protest against the prevailing culture from which its members originated.

Such counter cultures appeared to be protesting against the nature of relationships in the social structures as a whole. Additionally, the discussion on the 'liberation' model indicated that the way in which power is exercised within Church structures could be called into question, in that in the West the latter had become aligned with the secular social structures. A link was suggested between theological trends which underpin authoritarian regimes and lack of self-esteem.

Allied to this was Alberigo's view on the effect the Church's developing structure had on its theological response to the potential threat from increasing poverty.

The comment that 'the myth of personal destiny, sanctioned by the will of God, shut out any prospect of a change in the social order'[119] suggests that this reluctance to challenge the status quo was being justified theologically. Thus, the structures of the Church, reflecting as they did those in society at large, were undermining the expressed teaching of the Church to care for people such as the poor and the outcast.

The rise of popular movements among the poor produced a reaction on the part of the rich and powerful who levelled two accusations against them:

> that of *envy* – 'revolutionary sin' – for wanting to be equal to the rich; and that of *heresy*, for preaching the reign of God on earth and insubordination to the authorities.[120]

This last comment, about insubordination being part of the 'heresy' of the poor, is a clear indication of a reversion to the Graeco-Roman notion of humility, as discussed by Klaus Wengst, and also of further attempts to justify the prevailing situation theologically.

Another facet of this is the comments of both Brueggemann and Alberigo concerning the ways in which the structure protects itself by controlling access to God. The structure develops a theology; that theology controls the threat from the margins not only by restricting direct access to God but by minimising the potential for creativity through its emphasis on sinfulness and unworthiness. In practice, the effects of this are borne out by the observations of practitioners such as Baars and Terruwe that people whose self-esteem is low are more likely to be subservient in their attitude to the exercise of power by authoritarian structures.

It has been suggested in Chapter III that recognition of the need for affirmation is crucial if the Church is to fulfil its responsibility towards those on the margins. The paradox, highlighted by the discussion on the pro-life movement as being 'pro-marginal' as well as anti-abortion, brought out a distinction between the way people who are marginalised in different ways are treated.

The use of 'cost-effective' criteria in selecting what work might be undertaken is another example of a discrepancy which runs counter to Christian teaching. Those 'clients' who have a good prognosis are more likely to receive help than those who do not. This was illustrated by the preliminary research prior to setting up the Birmingham project in that it became apparent that those without family or community support to help their recovery following rehabilitation tended to be turned away. Yet, from a gospel perspective, they should have been to the forefront of concern.

Seen in the light of the broad understanding of what it means to be 'pro-life', agencies who have to make decisions based on cost-effective criteria may be at variance with that. Their decisions are not based on the intrinsic worth of the person, but on his/her social and economic potential. Those are the very criteria on which the future of an unwanted pregnancy may be decided.

There needs to be a reappraisal of the pro-life movement both by those within and by those Christians who, while not being actively involved in it, aim at solidarity with marginal people. On the one hand, the former need to consider the statement they are making, and that the most logical step is to take their campaigning beyond birth to those whom society would reject. At least one pro-life organisation has a section which is concerned with people with disabilities, on the basis of similar reasoning. But this needs to extend beyond those disadvantaged physically or mentally to those disadvantaged *socially*.

On the other hand, those who aim for solidarity with the marginalised might consider the underlying implications. It is indeed a struggle against the injustices they may suffer, but it is also an affirmation of the worth of each individual in the sight of God, regardless of his/her status and potential in the eyes of the world. To me there is an irony in that there are people who will spare themselves nothing when it comes to fighting for the rights of society's most disadvantaged, but who do not extend the struggle to the unborn. I personally find it difficult to pinpoint the moment when that God-given life came into being other than at conception.

The above comments highlight a disparity between the status of the human being before and after birth, and some disparity between categories of people after birth. I realise different people might explain this in different ways, but I would suggest one explanation lies in the question as to who is, and who is not, seen as a threat. The unborn and those with certain impairments do not present the same threat as the articulate marginal person who speaks out against the social-conditions that placed him or her there.

How, when, and why such threats are perceived is determined by the relationship between those in the structures and those on the margins of society. Following the views of Turner and Douglas, a paradox became apparent in that it is the marginal state itself which holds the key to equilibrium in the wider structures.

According to Turner, the dialectic between communitas and structure was essential to this; according to Douglas, there is power from the margins when the structures are open. Looking at Brueggemann's analysis of the biblical pattern of relationships in the light of this, it appeared that once the 'alternative' community of Moses had become established in the Promised Land, the dialectic was not maintained, and a hierarchical structure emerged.

Dialectic with the marginal state was replaced by conflict, the situation only being reversed by the birth of Jesus. Taking Wengst's views of the re-emergence of the Graeco-Roman understanding of humility, the pendulum then began to swing back towards a hierarchical structure, with the above effect.

For Turner, there were two aspects to the relationships which took place in 'communitas' and which maintained equilibrium. They were the absence of status and possessions.

With regard to status, Turner's concept of the role reversal of 'communitas' has been reduced to symbolic gestures in modern institutions. The example given of the coronation of British monarchs, who prior to anointing, are stripped of anything of value and dressed in a plain white robe is taken from the coronation of kings of Israel.

But the practice of sending people into what is in effect a liminal phase, from which they return to the structures revitalised, is one which is finding expression in training for Christian work. In some places trainees for Christian work spend a period of time as part of the homeless scene.[121] That this has the potential to affect the Churches is demonstrated by a student on placement in the Birmingham project; in his report he speaks of the following steps which need to be taken.

A) First the challenging and then the changing of the attitudes within the Church

B) Leaving the comfort and the security of the Church building to challenge and change the attitudes the community has towards these marginalised.[122]

A comment by Guiseppe Alberigo is relevant to this desire for security. In *The People of God in the Experience of Faith* he states that all the baptised 'need to be prepared to renounce an imposed uniformity and the false, though consoling, feeling of security'[123] that the structure gives, in order to undertake a thorough and faithful search for the ways in which the Spirit speaks to the Churches.

While a collective undertaking of this exercise of role reversal might be difficult, its extension would be likely to have an effect by producing leaders who had undergone this experience.

Status is linked to wealth. A key factor in the development of a hierarchical structure in the Church, according to Alberigo, was the growth of ecclesiastical wealth which led to an increasing autonomy of *ordo clericorum* to whom the availability and use of this wealth were guaranteed exclusively.[124]

The Church of England's financial crisis in the early 1990s precipitated discussions as to how this dependence upon wealth, and hence on outside financial institutions, might be reduced.

Martin Wroe, writing in *The Observer*, describes an interesting development in a Cambridgeshire parish.[125] The incumbent, who is unpaid and has a full-time job, is reported as saying that the Church should revert to former times when a bishop was spiritual adviser, parishes were self-reliant and clergy were unpaid. Such a discussion, following the repercussions of the Church Commissioners' financial losses on the property market, renders the views of Gilbert Shaw and Kenneth Leech concerning the 'Dark Night' of institutions, prophetic in both senses.

The views of the Cambridgeshire incumbent point to a model of Church, in which there is local autonomy and less distinction between clergy and laity. This resembles Alberigo's description of the early Church when, in his view, there had been less such distinction. Ordination did not mean an addition to the overall body of clergy, but the appointment to an office within the community who acted as a whole choosing those to guide them. 'The only distinction was between the Church and the world.'[126]

A significant change occurred after this when, following the ending of persecution, and hence a change in the relationship between Church and State, 'the eschatological expectation and the feeling of being "strangers" in society' was weakened.[127]

It is therefore this 'eschatological expectation' which needs to be recaptured. Without that basic motivation, any attempt to reform the Church's structures would be but a cosmetic exercise. The desert was, as Kenneth Leech points out, the way in which the Church kept alive that eschatological expectation of being strangers. According to him, 'The original Christian marginal rebel movement was that of the fourth-century desert monks'. At the beginning of the Constantinian establishment of Christianity, they took to the desert where 'they kept alive the vision of the new age through the centuries of darkness'.[128]

He sees that marginal people have a role in a present day equivalent. In his view, there needs to be a coming together of what he calls 'the rebel groups within and on the edge of the Churches, secular socialists, and the movements of the oppressed who form the new underclass in the cities' to find ways of working together. It is in this process of collaboration that the Christian rebel tradition may well rediscover its identity and find that it has a relationship with many people outside the institutional Church. This, he believes, could be 'a truly liberating experience and perhaps the beginning of a new phase of struggle'.[129]

That potential alliance is one to which I can relate. I often find that I have more in common with people in various counter-cultures than I have with traditional church-goers when it comes to social issues and the underlying spirituality.

The potential for this to be worked out in practice was demonstrated in Chapter V, with the examples of those who had found ways of uniting with the 'underclass'. What was significant was that this desert experience was not only affecting individuals, but also Churches and religious communities. For some, such as the New Mexico community, this is primarily one of expressing solidarity; but there are those, such as Austin Smith and the East Harlem Church, for whom solidarity moves from suffering with to struggling with the marginalised.

But such potential could, in theory, be curtailed by the individuals', or groups', dependence upon the wider structures. If the latter recognises a threat, it has the capacity to control whether the solidarity remains at a level of suffering with, or moves on to that of struggling with those on the margins. For example, funding by the parent body could be curtailed, therefore some degree of economic autonomy is needed.

A development, described in *Readers' Digest* in October 1993[130] recounted how Emmaus, an organisation where homeless single people live together in community, demonstrates the feasibility of this. They have land on which they raise vegetables and chickens; they take in discarded items, such as broken furniture, repair them for sale at a price people on low incomes can afford, and produce other items according to the talents of the community's members. Once up and running such communities are self-supporting.

This development is similar to the communes set up by Catholic anarchists and represents a fulfilment of the aspirations of the groups of young people encountered by the Birmingham project. Such a model could provide a degree of economic autonomy which would minimise dependence upon, and control by, wider structures.

Emmaus is ostensibly a secular body, although it has its origins in the work of the French priest Abbé Pierre among the rag pickers of Paris, and its name derives from the account of the disciples meeting Jesus on the road to Emmaus after the Resurrection. The name suggests a journeying together and community members are referred to as 'companions'. There are other groups which are also based on building self-supporting communities, but many of these groups are building community *for*, not *with*, marginal people and therefore may be less open to dialogue.

What is needed are communities which include a cross-section of people; some obviously marginal, others being people from the Churches who wish to gain from the experience of living in community with them. This happens to some extent with L'Arche, the communities formed by Jean Vanier which include people with severe 'learning difficulties', and others who give a year or two to be part of such communities. Were this to happen in other spheres, people from the Churches would be placed in a position where they could hear, through daily sharing, the situation of marginal people, and recognise the way that situation challenges the Churches.

The question is whether there are religious groups which have attained a comparable degree of economic independence to Emmaus, and hence freedom to develop new models of Christian community. Were this to be the case, such models might have the potential to redress the theological trends which have underpinned negative attitudes to marginal people. Such 'alternative communities' could, like the farming communes of the Catholic anarchists, fulfil the role that monasticism attempted to fill in the early Church, by being places of solidarity with marginal people and of reflection on the resulting challenges.

This could be a truly incarnational approach. It would be a way back to a spirituality which recognises the relationship between the human race and the created world, through its dependence upon its own resources, not outside financial institutions, and the creativity of its individual members. The latter in particular could contribute to restoring self-esteem.

Therefore those on the margins have the potential to recall those in the Church to its roots. Voluntary marginality, it is suggested, is the biblical pattern of relationships and the place from which prophets speak; involuntary marginality is the indicator that there are dysfunctional factors at work in society. Taken together, there is the potential for restoring the prophetic role of the Church. Kenneth Leech, in discussing the 'corporate Dark Night', refers to the purification needed to take us back to root principles. The 'urban jungle', it is contended, can be such a place of purification, not only for individuals, but for the Church as a whole.

Aloysius Pieris' statement, concerning the 'magisterium of the poor' discussed at the end of the last chapter, brings the poor, and marginal person from their place on the margins to a key role in the Churches. That can be a reality if we have the vision to create situations, or communities, in which it be expressed.

Notes

1. Since then there have been efforts, including provision in the 1989 Children Act, and projects undertaken by voluntary agencies to redress this and provide after-care for young people up to twenty-one years old. But in practice shortage of resources has meant that this has done little more than scratch the surface. The overall problem of young people without supportive families remains.

2. See Vincent Donovan, *The Church in the Midst of Creation,* New York, 1989.

3. For example, Paul speaks of himself as an apostle to the Gentiles (Romans 11:13).

4. J. Hoekendijk, *The Church Inside Out*, London, 1967, p.64

5. 'Street kids' typically come from broken homes, then drift into various forms of substance abuse, according to Dave Cave of the Anfield Road Fellowship. See Margaret Hebblethwaite *Basic is Beautiful,* London 1993. Eileen Carroll, a religious sister who works with street people in Leeds, refers in privately circulated newsletters to the loneliness and lack of self-worth among the street people she knows; this is not explicitly linked to the kind of childhood rejection described above, but from conversations with her, the backgrounds are similar.

6. 'Psychological homelessness' is a particularly helpful term used by Rex Ambler in 'Vagrancy', an open lecture at St Francis Hall, Birmingham University, 7 October 1971. It demonstrates the wider social factors affecting those on the streets. He recognises that the visible problem of being without a home or job is only half the problem. They feel isolated from the mainstream of society, do not believe that they belong anywhere or to anyone, or if they once did, they have now been rejected.

7. Haddon Willmer, *Poverty in the New Testament and in Britain Today*, Theology of Peace Conference, Bradford University, 1988.

8. *Alcohol and Alcoholism;* Report of a Special Committee of The Royal College of Psychiatrists, London, 1979, p.67.

9. Kenneth Leech *What Everyone Should Know about Drugs,* London, 1983, p.50.

10. Kenneth Leech *Keep the Faith Baby,* London, 1973, pp 35-36.
11. Conrad W Baars & Anna Terruwe, *Healing the Unaffirmed: Recognizing Deprivation Neurosis,* New York, 1976. Chapter 1, 'Why so many neurotics fail to respond to psychiatric treatment', identifies the condition which Baars and Terruwe describe as 'deprivation neurosis'; chapter 6, 'What kind of therapy do deprivation neurotics need?' as the title suggests, goes into the kind of treatment needed.
12. Chad Varah, *The Samaritans: Befriending the Suicidal,* London, Revised Edition, 1987, Introduction.
13. Kenneth Leech, *Care and Conflict,* London, 1990, p.29.
14. *Care and Conflict,* pp 27-29.
15. Mary Beasley, *Back from the Brink* Oxford, 1982.
16. Jean Vanier, *The Broken Body* London, 1988, pp.78-79.
17. Deuteronomy 10:19.
18. Luke 4.
19. Leonardo Boff, *St Francis: A Model for Human Liberation,* London, 1985, p.1.
20. St John Ervine, *God's Soldier: General William Booth,* London, 1934, p.38.
21. Robert Sandall, *The History of the Salvation Army* Vol I, London, 1947, p.66.
22. W. T. Stead, *General Booth* London, 1891, p 50.
23. *General Booth,* p.50.
24. Margaret Hebblethwaite, *Basic is Beautiful,* London, 1993, p.174.
25. *Basic is Beautiful,* p.165.
26. *Basic is Beautiful,* p.141.
27. Margaret Walsh, *Here's Hoping,* Sheffield, 1991, p.10.
28. *Basic is Beautiful,* p.159.
29. Vincent Donovan, *Christianity Rediscovered,* New York, p.vii.
30. see E. P. Thompson, *The Making of the English Working Class* London, 1980, p.392.
31. Robert Schreiter, *Constructing Local Theologies,* London, 1976, pp.12-15.
32. Royal College of Psychiatrists, *Alcohol and Alcoholism,* London, 1979.
33. Conrad W. Baars & Anna Terruwe, *Healing the Unaffirmed: Recognizing Deprivation Neurosis,* New York, 1976, pp.109-110.
34. Gerard W. Hughes, S.J., *God of Surprises,* London, 1985, p.34.
35. *God of Surprises* p.38.
36. Elaine Pagels, *Adam, Eve, and the Serpent* London, 1988, p.98.

37. *Adam, Eve, and the Serpent* p.113.

38. *Adam, Eve, and the Serpent* p.xxvi.

39. Richard P. McBrien, *Catholicism,* London, 1984, p.165.

40. Karl Rahner (ed), *Encyclopaedia of Theology: A Concise Sacramentum Mundi,* London, 1975, p.1151.

41. *Servants of Christ's Mission,* from papers of the 34th general council of the Society of Jesus, p.6.

42. *Healing the Unaffirmed,* p.73.

43. These comments are based my visits to the communities attached to the Church of the Redeemer, Houston, Texas, and that at Ann Arbor, Michigan, in 1974.

44. *Minjung Theology: People as the Subjects of History*, papers edited by the Commission on Theological Concerns of the Christian Conference of Asia, 1983. Introduction, p.xvii.

45. David Suh Kwang-Sun, Korean Theological Development in *Minjung Theology: People as the Subjects of History,* p.42.

46. Ahn Byung Mu, Jesus and the Minjung in the Gospel of Mark in *Minjung Theology: People as the Subjects of History,* p.138ff.

47. Suh Nam-dong, Towards a Theology of Han in *Minjung Theology: People as the Subjects of History,* p.58.

48. Suh Nam-dong, Towards a Theology of Han in *Minjung Theology: People as the Subjects of History,* pp. 64-65.

49. Moon Hee-suk Cyris, An Old Testament Understanding of Minjung, in *Minjung Theology: People as the Subjects of History,* p.128.

50. J Russell Chandran, *A Methodological Approach to Third World Theology, The Irruption of the Third World: Challenge to Theology* papers from the fifth International Conference of the Ecumenical Association of Third World Theologians, 17-29 August, 1981, New Delhi, India, edited by Virginia Fabella and Sergio Torres, New York, 1983, p.80.

51. Sarah Lonsdale writing in *The Observer*, 30 August, 1992.

52. Kenneth Leech, *True God*, London, 1985, p.251.

53. Leonard I. Krimerman, and Lewis Perry (Editors), *Patterns of Anarchy: A collection of writings on the anarchist tradition,* New York, 1966, p.375.

54. The Green Revolution *Patterns of Anarchy: A collection of writings on the anarchist tradition,* p.377.

55. I Peter 5:5.

56. Colin Ward, *Anarchy in Action,* London, 1982, p.28.

57. *Anarchy in Action,* p.32.

58. See chapter IV.

59. *Patterns of Anarchy,* p.51.
60. *The Tablet,* 12 December 1992.
61. G. A. Gaskell, *Dictionary of Scripture and Myth,* New York, 1988, p.288.
62. John Saward *Perfect Fools,* London, 1980, pp 41-42.
63. Victor W. Turner, *The Ritual Process,* London,1969, pp 95-6.
64. ibid., pp.97.
65. op.cit., p 129.
66. op.cit., p.109.
67. see the chapter on Marginality in Hastings, Adrian, *The Faces of God,* London, 1975.
68. *A Dictionary of Symbols,* p.315.
69. Genesis 32:24,25.
70. Adrian Hastings, *The Faces of God* pp 18-19.
71. Mary Douglas, *Purity and Danger,* London, 1966, p.97.
72. *Purity and Danger* pp 112-113.
73. For example, Erving Goffman.
74. Walter Brueggemann *The Prophetic Imagination,* London, 1978, p.16.
75. ibid. p.19.
76. op.cit. p.28.
77. op.cit. Chapter I sets the discussion on the alternative community against the background of the Exodus; one explicit reference to this is the 'wilderness theme' is on p.27.
78. op.cit. pp.32-33.
79. op.cit. p.38.
80. op.cit. p.30.
81. op.cit. p.39.
82. op.cit. p.35.
83. Guiseppe Alberigo *The People of God (Le Popolo di Dio) in the Experience of Faith* (Concilium: La Iglesia Popular: Between Fear and Hope. eds Leonardo Boff & Virgin Elizonda Tr., Edinburgh, 1984, No. 176), p.28 .
84. Wengst supports this with references from the prophet Amos 2.10, 3.1, 9.7, 7.1-6, 5.8f, 9.5ff.
85. Zephaniah 3.11 and 2.3.
86. Proverbs 16.19.
87. Klaus Wengst, *Humility: the Solidarity of the Humiliated,* London, 1988, p.47.
88. ibid., p.53.
89. op.cit., p.57.
90. op.cit., p.58.
91. op.cit., p.58.

92. See note 30.
93. *Care and Conflict,* p.33.
94. *Perfect Fools,* pp.68-9.
95. *Perfect Fools,* pp.40-42.
96. *Care and Conflict,* p.72.
97. *Dictionary of Scripture and Myth*, p.814.
98. Benedicta Ward and Norman Russell, *The Lives of the Desert Fathers*, Oxford, 1980, p.16.
99. David Jenkins, *The Contradiction of Christianity,* London, 1976, p.49.
100. *Perfect Fools,* pp.68-69.
101. see for example Nicky Cruz with Jamie Buckingham, *Run Baby Run: The Story of Nicky Cruz*, Hodder, 1968, and Cookie Rodriguez with Betty Schonauer, *Please Make Me Cry*, New York, 1974.
102. Maria Boulding (ed), *A Touch of God: Eight Monastic Journeys*, London, 1982, p.151.
103. *From Addiction to Liberation* by Mary Beasley and Dom John Bolton, O.S.B., *Signum*, 4 August 1989, Vol. 17 No 15, London.
104. Austin Smith, *Passion for the Inner City*, London, 1983, p.67.
105. ibid. p.68.
106. op. cit p.98.
107. *The Contemplative Life in the Urban Desert*, Fairacres Chronicle, Vol. 14 No. 3.
108. The Prophetic Role of Monasticism, *Desert Call*, Vol. 28, No. 3, 1993.
109. Thomas Merton, *Contemplation in a World of Action,* New York, 1973, p 232.
110. ibid. p 236.
111. *The Asian Journal of Thomas Merton,* Sheldon, 1974, p.329.
112. *Care and Conflict,* p.74.
113. *The People of God,* p.25.
114. Bruce Kenrick, *Come out the Wilderness,* London, 1962, p.145.
115. From an unpublished transcript of a talk Aloysius Pieris gave to a conference of religious in Ireland.
116. see Revelation in the Jewish tradition in *The Levinas Reader,* edited by Sean Hand, Oxford, 1989.
117. see note 16.
108. A cult which originated in California in the 1960s; it had its roots in the Jesus Movement, but later moved away from orthodox Christianity, becoming known for its practice of 'hookers for Jesus'.

109. *The People of God (Le Popolo di Dio) in the Experience of Faith,* p.165.
120. ibid., p.176.
121. Verbal accounts have been given of two Anglican dioceses where this has been incorporated into training programmes.
122. Placement report by John McFarlane, Pastoral Studies course, Birmingham University.
123. *The People of God (Le Popolo di Dio) in the Experience of Faith* p.36.
124. ibid., pp.26-27.
125. The Church in Crisis, *The Observer*, 20 February 1994.
126. *The People of God (Le Popolo di Dio) in the Experience of Faith* p.25.
127. ibid., p.25.
128. *Care and Conflict* p.127.
190. ibid. p.128.
130. Tim Bouquet, *Where Down and Outs Get Up and Go,* Readers' Digest, October 1993.

Appendix
The Twelve Steps of Alcoholics Anonymous

We

1. Admitted we were powerless over alcohol – that our lives had become unmanageable
2. Came to believe that a Power greater than ourselves could restore us to sanity
3. Made a decision to turn our will and our lives over to the care of God as we understood Him
4. Made a searching and fearless moral inventory of ourselves
5. Admitted to God, to ourselves, and to another human being, the exact nature of our wrongs
6. Were entirely ready to have God remove all these defects of character
7. Humbly asked Him to remove our shortcomings
8. Made a list of all persons we had harmed and became willing to make amends to them all
9. Made direct amends to such people wherever possible, except when to do so would injure them or others
10. Continued to take a personal inventory and when we were wrong promptly admitted it
11. Sought through power of prayer and meditation to improve our conscious contact with God as we understood Him, praying only for knowledge of His will for us and the power to carry that out
12. Having a spiritual experience as a result of these steps, tried to carry this message to alcoholics and to practise these principles in all our affairs.